MW00825097

"I AM ..."

STORYTELLING IN WORSHIP

"I AM ..."

STORYTELLING IN WORSHIP

MONOLOGUES AND DRAMATIC READINGS

Slayden A. Yarbrough

New Harbor Press

Copyright © 2020 Slayden A. Yarbrough

All rights reserved. No part of this publication may be reproduced, distributed or transmitted in any form or by any means, including photocopying, recording, or other electronic or mechanical methods, without the prior written permission of the publisher, except in the case of brief quotations embodied in critical reviews and certain other noncommercial uses permitted by copyright law. For permission requests, write to the publisher, addressed "Attention: Permissions Coordinator," at the address below.

New Harbor Press
1601 Mt Rushmore Rd, Ste 3288
Rapid City, SD 57701
www.newharborpress.com

Ordering Information:
Quantity sales. Special discounts are available on quantity purchases by corporations, associations, and others. For details, contact the "Special Sales Department" at the address above.

"I Am ..." Storytelling in Worship/Yarbrough —1st ed.

ISBN 978-1-63357-339-0
First edition: 10 9 8 7 6 5 4 3 2 1

Scripture quotations marked "NASB" are taken from the NEW AMERICAN STANDARD BIBLE®, Copyright © 1960, 1962, 1963, 1968, 1971, 1972, 1973, 1975, 1977, 1995 by The Lockman Foundation. Used by permission.

Scripture quotations marked "NIV" are taken from THE HOLY BIBLE, NEW INTERNATIONAL VERSION®, NIV® Copyright © 1973, 1978, 1984, 2011 by Biblica, Inc.® Used by permission. All rights reserved worldwide.

DEDICATED TO

Janis, soulmate and proofreader for more than fifty-five years.

Scott, son and director who helped me see that faith and drama ask the same questions.

Kellan, grandson from whom I have inherited the earth and the future.

Contents

PREFACE

During my twenty-two years as a religion professor at Oklahoma Baptist University, I often served as an interim pastor for churches in the state during times of transition between pastors. One of the churches I served was First Baptist Church of Pawnee. For those of you who might remember hearing of him, the city was the home of the Wild West show entertainer Pawnee Bill.

First Baptist Church had worship services on Sunday morning and evening. One Sunday evening I had prepared a sermon on Peter. With a few hours to go before worship began, I decided that instead of "preaching" from my outline, I would simply present myself as Peter and tell my story. I incorporated all of my planned content and had an unscripted conversation with the congregation. The people really seemed to enjoy the monologue approach, as I got numerous positive comments afterward. I didn't prepare a full manuscript, as I do for most of my sermons and monologues when speaking in churches, so "Peter" simply went into the unwritten archives of my presentations.

During my years teaching Old Testament and New Testament History and Literature at Oklahoma Baptist University, I became convinced that Christians and students of the Bible needed to have an understanding of the development of the canon, the text, and the translations of the Scriptures in order to have a solid foundation for interpretation. But I was also looking for an approach to presenting this material in churches that would not sound like a boring lecture.

In those days I usually attended the annual meeting of the Southern Baptist Historical Society. One year one of the speakers was well-known Baptist historian Walter "Buddy" Shurden. He presented a monologue as the Bible. I really liked his approach. I borrowed the concept and wrote my own monologue, which I called "I Am the Bible."

Later on, new ideas came to mind for creative ways to present the lives and stories of biblical and historical characters, as well as important events. In these instances, I decided to manuscript my stories and preserve them for use at future times. Having served as pulpit supply or interim pastor in many churches during my teaching career and retirement years, I have thoroughly enjoyed playing the role of storyteller to congregations who seem to appreciate the variety my monologues provide. I have enjoyed creating new characters and stories and revisiting previous ones as new insights come to mind. The collection that follows is a result of my efforts. Hopefully you will find these monologues thoughtful, challenging, and entertaining.

As you read this book of monologue and dramatic reading presentations, I hope you will be inspired to develop your own favorite characters. You will find satisfaction from getting into the minds of your characters, and you will be delighted at the response of your hearers as they connect their personal biblical and historical journeys with the characters you are presenting.

Special thanks goes to Janis for laboriously proofreading the manuscript and making numerous editorial suggestions to make it more accurate and readable; to Dr. Warren McWilliams and Dr. Mike Kuykendall, two good friends who read and made excellent suggestions for these stories; and to the many members of the congregations who participated and contributed superb changes to the characters these stories present. Finally, thanks to my American Baptist Churches TIM group (Together in Ministry), who at our monthly meetings encouraged me to be active in my retirement, affirmed my dreams, and served as a sounding board for some of the ideas in this volume.

INTRODUCTION

A familiar phrase in the Scriptures is "I am." In the story of the experience of Moses and the burning bush, God is portrayed as identifying himself as *YHWH*, which can be translated "I am who I am." In the Gospel of John there are seven "I am" sayings of Jesus. Jesus is recorded as saying "I am the bread of life," "the light of the world," "the door," "the good shepherd," "the resurrection and the life," "the way and the truth and the life," and "the vine." First-person statements are a unique way of characterizing the identity of the speaker and conveying important understandings of the subject.

Monologues capture the attention of an audience in a unique way by engaging the hearers or readers in a dialogue with the subject or presenter. In 1970, the movie *Patton* opened with George C. Scott as Gen. George S. Patton appearing and speaking before the Third Army in front of a huge American flag. The abbreviated version of his speech was given several times leading up to the invasion of Europe on D-Day, including on June 5, 1944. Patton's powerful deliverance inspired and motivated the troops readying for battle even though they would not be a part of the D-Day invasion. I came away from the movie feeling I had been present for Patton's monologue. For the moment I was convinced it was Patton speaking, not that year's Academy Award winner for Best Actor.

Other famous actors in one-man shows have left an impression on me. They brought me into the presence of historical figures like Harry Truman, portrayed by Gary Sinese, and Mark Twain, presented by Hal Holbrook. These performances stirred my imagination and enabled me to appreciate the power of monologues to teach and engage audiences in dialogue with important figures from our history, stories, and even legends.

Monologues and dramatic readings are basically storytelling. In the 1980s, when I was a university religion professor, a movement called "narrative theology" emphasized the importance of storytelling in the Bible. I found the approach most helpful in interpreting Scripture. A story is a dramatic tool to convey understanding, identity, and a collective memory that connects generations. Stories are a way to understand God, to unite individuals into communities, and to remember heroes and villains of the past in order to respond to the challenges of the present. Drama is a wonderful teacher as we seek to understand who we are, both individually and collectively. Stories stir the imagination, connecting the past with the present—and often the future—on a personal level.

Stories of creation, of the journeys of the patriarchs, judges, and deliverers, and of kings and prophets illuminate the pages of the Hebrew Bible, or the Old Testament. In the New Testament there are all of the numerous and wonderful stories of the earthly ministry of Jesus and his followers. In fact, Jesus himself had a reputation as a marvelous storyteller. His use of parables to convey important understandings of life, faith, and friendship continue to be models of teaching that reveal profound and common-sense truths.

I taught courses in Bible, church history, denominational history, and a variety of religious subjects at the university level for twenty-nine years. During this time, I developed a significant core of background and resource materials from both the Scriptures and the history of Christianity for use in sermons. This information was invaluable as I began to prepare sermons and dramatic presentations for church audiences in the form of first-person monologues. I am not the first person to use the technique of monologues, but I have discovered some unique tools that make monologue presentations an enjoyable, effective way to present familiar stories, while at the same time engaging and challenging hearers to participate in the story and apply its lessons.

I often present my hearers with a question about a biblical character. For example, if I am speaking on Peter, I might ask the congregation, "If you had a choice of reading a story about Peter as he met the women coming from the tomb on the Sunday after the burial of Jesus, or of actually hearing Peter tell the story, which would you prefer?" I think the answer is obvious. The listeners would rather hear Peter tell of his excitement upon hearing the good news that Jesus was not in the tomb; of how the women had shared their emotional responses with him; of his eagerness to see for himself by racing to the place where the body of Jesus had been laid. Although Peter cannot actually be with us, he can be dramatically present through the telling of his story in a monologue presentation.

First-person monologues and dramatic readings are creative ways of storytelling. Standing before an audience, sharing the story of your character or characters in the first person, asking questions for your listeners to consider, getting them to engage their imaginations, taking them to another time and place in their minds, and encouraging them to apply the lessons learned from the past to the contemporary world is a delightful experience.

As I prepare a monologue, I seek to paint the historical, religious, or literary world of the character I am presenting. What is going on in the Jewish and Roman historical, cultural, political, and geographical scene? The character then frames the presentation by asking the questions that matter to him or her in light of the specific issues, challenges, opportunities, and other personalities that make up the story. I will often create ideas, thoughts, and scenarios that may not have appeared in the original account, but which seem to make sense in the telling of the story.

I use the monologue format to ask the hearers what they are thinking, how they are responding, what they might do, and whether they like or even agree with what the character is saying. I try to provide as much information as I can about the character or topic, and hopefully, enable the hearers to identify with the character as he or she debates, learns from, and struggles with the issues arising in the story.

I usually don't use costumes in my monologues. One exception is when I present "A Visit from Martin Luther," a monologue I have prepared for Reformation Sunday in which I often wear a simple black robe similar to what a monk might have worn in the sixteenth century, but in general, I leave costuming up to the imagination of the listeners. However, I have prepared a few dramatic readings for participation by members of the congregation, and they often like to dress in period or character costumes. I have readings for the Christmas season and the Passion Week in which costumes are in order for volunteers. Many churches have a supply of costumes available for use that reflect the biblical period, if the presenter prefers to dress the part.

One of my major goals is to teach the hearers, to enable them to learn from the first-person narrative, to take them beyond a simple sermon or lecture and into the life and world of the character. I attempt to lead listeners to evaluate their own stories, to consider how they identify with the character before them. And to be honest, I try to entertain them. I use humor, seriousness, self-deprecation, contemplations, and exaggeration to keep the audience engaged. In so doing I create interesting characters. I allow myself creative license in the telling of my story. I seek to make my hearers laugh and smile; feel sorrow or loss, anger or excitement. In the end, I want them to depart believing for a moment that they have been in the presence of someone from the past.

In this short volume I am including six monologue stories and three dramatic readings. "I Am the Bible" is a wonderful way to tell the history of "the Book"—significant aspects and challenges of the Scriptures—without simply giving a lecture on topics such as canon, text, and translations. I have presented this monologue almost sixty times over the years, as I attempt to have the written Word become incarnate, so to speak, in the twenty-first century. I have revised this monologue time and time again over the years to make it continuously relevant, including references to the use of electronic devices with Bible apps, updating the progress and availability of new translations in languages of the peoples of the earth, and the publication of new translations as they appear. I always receive positive results from this presentation. I even wrote words for a hymn that congregations usually sing, entitled "Eternal Word, O Word of God," where I convey the Word as creative, incarnate, proclaimed, written, and lived. The hymn fits well with the monologue approach.

For a number of years, I have wanted to do a monologue on John Mark and the writing of the first Gospel. After completing my final draft for this book, I decided to go ahead with my plan in order to include it in this volume. Therefore, I wrote "I Am John Mark and I Wrote the First Gospel." The monologue takes the position that Mark was eminently qualified to write a gospel of Jesus. He had at least four significant influences in his life: his mother, his uncle Barnabas, Paul, and Peter, and he knew many of the other apostles. His special relationship as the amanuensis for Peter was of most importance, as he carefully transcribed the apostle's sermons. The church faced a critical time when Mark authored his Gospel, which would go on to provide a foundation for Matthew and Luke. His story should inspire all of us to examine our skills and to appreciate those who have influenced us in our respective journeys.

Using the parable by Jesus of the father and two sons in Luke 15, I enjoy presenting two monologues in successive services. The first is the "Prodigal Son," who tells his story from the perspective of the adventuresome but wayward second-born. This story includes touches of humor and reflection throughout the wayward son's journey. In the second service I present the parable from the eyes of the older brother, whose story is also important and who is frequently cast, simply and unfairly, as the bad guy. In this story I have also included a visit from the father, whose parental love transcends the diverse nature of his two sons.

My journey of interpretation of the Book of Revelation led me to prepare and present a monologue I call "John and the Apocalypse." In this reading I present the historical, or what is often called the amillennial view of Revelation. Many congregations are not familiar with this interpretation. Many ministers in the twenty-first century, like those of previous generations, simply avoid the book. But I find this monologue to be a didactic way of presenting my interpretation of the book—namely, that it was written in apocalyptic imagery to provide the readers with protection from persecution by Roman officials. This approach makes the Book of Revelation relevant for any generation, including the twenty-first century church.

I am a church historian. My favorite character in church history—outside heroes of my own denomination—is Martin Luther. Years ago, on Reformation Sunday, I was asked by a local congregation where I had served as interim pastor to speak on Luther. I prepared a monologue and have been editing it for more than twenty-five years. I love to do this presentation. I find Luther to be a character with whom so many of us can identify as we struggle with our own understanding along our faith journeys. And, the audience gets to learn some significant church history. They get to sense the fear of political and religious opponents, know the joy and satisfaction of discovering one's own faith through the freedom of questioning established norms, and even laugh at times.

I have also prepared three dramatic readings for this volume. I refer to these as dramatic readings because I ask members of the congregation to participate by assigning each of them a character from the story. In smaller churches it is hard to find people willing or courageous enough to learn their lines, so I allow them to read their parts (with feeling, of course). Many decide to memorize their lines. I also encourage the readers to freely edit their characters' lines to align them with their own personalities and understanding. Some have been really creative, and I often revise my text to incorporate their respective versions. I have never been disappointed in their creativity. Obviously, there is a lot of "ham" in most of us, and this comes out in these presentations

The first dramatic reading is called "I Am Christmas." I have been doing this drama in churches for approximately thirty years. In fact, since my interim pastorates sometimes cover two Advent seasons, I have found that some congregations want to repeat the performance in back-to-back Christmases. On one occasion a church invited me back to lead the presentation of "I Am Christmas." This reading, along with "Voices from the Passion Week," is suitable for any size congregation but is especially useful for smaller congregations that are limited in their options of Christmas programs that don't involve people with special musical or dramatic skills.

I have continuously revised the "I Am Christmas" presentation over the years by editing and adding characters. My current list of nine characters includes Augustus Caesar, Elizabeth, Bethlehem (yes, you can do places), the star (yes, you can include inanimate objects), Mary, shepherds in the field, the wise men, and Herod the Great. I even include the congregation at the end of the program to enable them to identify with Christmas. There is also a narrator (usually the pastor), who reads Scripture and frames the presentation, as well as presenting a challenge following the characters' presentations.

Furthermore, I have prepared an order of worship which intersperses appropriate verses from familiar Christmas carols to be sung between characters' presentations. The program usually takes forty-five minutes to an hour and is a fun way to present the Christmas story. Involving so many of the congregants is a wonderful way to use the talents of a selective group of people, and the program is always well-received. If a church lacks a large choir to present a Christmas cantata, "I Am Christmas" is an alternate way to tell the Christmas story.

A second dramatic reading, called "Voices from the Passion Week," takes the congregation through the last week in the earthly ministry of Jesus up through his burial. Again, I tell the story through several characters. Currently, the presentation includes Mary, her sister Martha, and the city of Jerusalem. I created Zachariah, a young boy who observes the entry of Jesus into the Jewish capital on Palm Sunday. I named the money changer Simeon, another invented and colorful character who humorously portrays the chaotic scene in the temple court. Other characters are John Mark, Caiaphas the high priest, the procurator Pontius Pilate, and Mary Magdalene. I wrote about the boy in order to include a part for a young member of a church where I was serving as interim pastor. His name was Zach and he was active in drama, so I named the character Zachariah. A narrator sets up the reading and brings it all together at the end.

Finally, I wrote a dramatic reading called "My Name Is Baptist but My Friends Call Me Liberty." I use it for July 4th services, but it could be appropriate at any time in a Baptist church. Characters include John Smyth, Thomas Helwys, Roger Williams, and John Leland. Their lives chart the history of Baptists from the movement's beginnings in Amsterdam through the adoption of the Constitution of the United States, the Bill of Rights, and the First Amendment. And I add a personal character for my contemporaries who I identify as Baptist. If you are not a Baptist, this presentation can encourage you to examine your own denomination and create a character or characters to highlight an identifying characteristic from your history.

My purpose in preparing this book is to provide my readers with examples of monologue sermons or dramatic readings that they can use in congregational worship. I hope pastors and worship leaders will be encouraged to write their own monologues and use this imaginative storytelling technique to make characters from the past come alive in a relevant way to the present. In so doing, they will realize this is a wonderful learning approach for themselves and their people, which will result in a unique way of proclaiming to the contemporary generation the good news from the heritage of faith.

Two other comments are necessary. I have had a few of these presentations published in the original versions. "I Am the Bible" and "I Am Christmas" were published in *Proclaim*, a ministers' journal. I received letters from pastors who had read my monologues, liked what I did, and used the presentations in their churches. "John and the Apocalypse" was also purchased for publication in *Proclaim*, but for some unknown reason was never published. The journal ceased publication a number of years ago.

Furthermore, I have edited and continue to edit each program before I present it. New insights and new churches inspire me to update my characters. Each preparation brings me joy on a personal level.

I hope you enjoy these monologues and dramatic readings. As you read them, try to envision the character speaking directly to you. As you do, enter into dialogue with the character. Feel free to edit these presentations for use in your congregations. You might even disagree with some of my interpretations. I encourage you to adapt the stories accordingly. Then apply what you learn from these monologues, preparing and delivering stories of your own, retelling the lives of new characters through them in the first person. Let the drama begin!!

MONOLOGUE 1: I AM THE BIBLE

<u>TEXTS:</u>
2 Timothy 3:16-17 (NIV)[1] – All Scripture is God-breathed and is useful for teaching, rebuking, correcting and training in righteousness, so that the servant of God may be thoroughly equipped for every good work.

2 Peter 3:15-16 – Bear in mind that our Lord's patience means salvation, just as our dear brother Paul also wrote you with the wisdom that God gave him. He writes the same way in all his letters, speaking in them of these matters. His letters contain some things that are hard to understand, which ignorant and unstable people distort, as they do the other Scriptures, to their own destruction.

<u>INTRODUCTION:</u>
Christians have an historic commitment to and love for the Bible. Its message has been the written source for faith and practice in thousands of languages for almost two millennia. At the same time, believers and nonbelievers have exerted an enormous amount of energy in an ongoing polemic over the Scriptures. In light of these circumstances, if it could talk—if the written Word could become incarnate—what would the Bible say to us today? I want you to use your creative imagination while I attempt to put myself in the role of the Bible and speak to you in a monologue presentation that tells you about the nature, the history, the purpose, and the place of the Bible in our lives. So, sit back and hear what the Bible has to say to you at this time.

MONOLOGUE: I AM THE BIBLE

Hello! I am the Bible. I would not be surprised if most of you, maybe all of you, own at least one copy of me. Some of you, possibly the majority of you, own multiple copies of me, and perhaps in different translations. And many of you now read me on your tablet or phone or some other electronic device. In fact, some preachers now read me during their sermons from an electronic tablet rather than a book. But most of you still prefer the good old book format, at least for now.

I come in many sizes. Some will fit into your pocket or purse. Others are so large one person would have a difficult time lifting up a single copy.

I come in many colors. There is basic black, which is the historic standard for preaching, teaching, and personal study. Snow white is wonderful for weddings. Revival red works great during evangelistic meetings. There are many other colors for my covers, including brown, blue, burgundy, Gideon green, and on and on to meet individual tastes.

My name comes from the Greek word *biblos*. It translates simply as "book." I am "the Book!"

Actually, in the Protestant tradition I am sixty-six books. Thirty-nine of my books are found in what you call the Old Testament, or the Hebrew Bible. Although the Hebrew Bible includes all of the thirty-nine writings in the Protestant list, its numbering results in only twenty-four. This is because books like 1 and 2 Samuel or 1 and 2 Kings are considered only one book each, and the twelve Minor Prophets are considered only one book, called the Twelve.

Twenty-seven of my writings comprise the New Testament. Each book has its own author and its own story with its own message and its own purpose. You study me by turning to specific chapters and verses, but it was not until the thirteenth century AD when I began to be divided for easier reading and study. In that century, Stephen Langton, archbishop of Canterbury, divided me into chapters for the first time. And it was not until the fifteenth and sixteenth centuries that my chapters were divided into verses. I must confess, these innovations are most helpful to my readers, wouldn't you agree? For example, if someone said, "Look up John 3:16," you could quickly find the verse. This is much faster than if I had remained without chapters and verses in my books and someone said, "Look up the verse in John where Nicodemus visits Jesus at night."

I am an old book. Some parts of me are over 3,000 years old. My latest parts are almost 2,000 years old. I won't tell you about space travel, nuclear physics, computers, iPods or tablets, cell phones or smart phones. But I will tell you about God, whose self-revelation is as contemporary as today's breaking news.

I am a product of the people of God. I was written by Hebrews, who produced my Old Testament, and by Christians (most of whom were Jews with the exception of the gentile Luke), who produced my New Testament. I was written to the people of God to help them understand who they are and what is expected of them.

I was initially preserved in collections to be used by the people of God. For example, in the Hebrew Bible, first came the Torah, which is also called the Law or the Pentateuch (the first five books of my Old Testament). Then the Prophets appeared, followed by the rest of the Writings, and they came together to form my Old Testament. Interestingly, you Christians divided the Prophets, the second section of my old book, into "History" and "the Prophets." But for the Hebrews, the books that appear to be history to you—Joshua, Judges, Samuel, and Kings—were seen as prophetic messages just as much as Isaiah, Jeremiah, Ezekiel, and the Twelve, which you call the Minor Prophets. But these "history" writings told how the Hebrews won the land of Canaan, settled there, and eventually lost the land. These books, which the Hebrew canon calls the Former Prophets, were both a prophetic warning and an encouragement for all of the later generations who would read them to learn from their nation's past.

The Latter Prophets included Isaiah, Jeremiah, Ezekiel, and the Twelve, or as Christians call them, the Minor Prophets. After the Prophets, both Former and Latter, the Writings were added. The Writings were divided into three parts: Poetry (Psalms, Proverbs, and Job), the Megillot (five rolls which were read at Jewish festivals: the Song of Songs, Ruth, Lamentations, Ecclesiastes, and Esther), the Chronicler's History (Ezra, Nehemiah, and 1 and 2 Chronicles), and Daniel.

I might also remind you that my Old Testament, or the Hebrew Bible, was being used authoritatively by God's people during and following the earthly ministry of Jesus. But it was not until around AD 90-100, in a small Palestinian town named Jamnia, it is believed, that a council of rabbis officially concluded that these and these books alone were the accepted books in the Hebrew canon.

My New Testament was written by Christians, to Christians, for Christians. Paul's letters were actually the first writings to appear that would become a part of my New Testament. In fact, 2 Peter 3:15-16 makes reference to "all of Paul's letters," which some were "twisting" to their own destruction. The writer also gave Paul's epistles authoritative status, comparing them to the "other Scriptures."

After Paul's writings the four Gospels began to appear. Why? Because eyewitnesses to the resurrected Jesus were dying off, both naturally and as martyrs. Jesus had not returned as expected. Furthermore, the church was being engulfed by numerous converts, mostly gentiles, who needed to be taught, and therefore there needed to be a record of the life and ministry of Jesus. The Gospels were followed by the other books, including Acts, the general letters, and the apocalyptic writing known as Revelation. Do you know it took over three hundred years for Christianity to finally say, "These are the accepted books," or in technical terms, the New Testament canon? The Greek word for "canon" means a measuring rod, or for those of you who sew, it can be seen as a yardstick, or a ruler.

I might point out that some Christians wanted to include other writings, like the Epistle of Barnabas, the Shepherd of Hermas, and the Didache (also known as the Teaching of the Twelve Apostles). Some Christians did not accept James, 2 Peter, Hebrews, or some of the other writings. In fact, the first time you had a complete list of the twenty-seven books of the New Testament, no more and no less, was not until AD 367, when Athanasius, the bishop or pastor of Alexandria in Egypt, prepared an annual Easter letter to his congregation. This is the first extant writing including the exact list of the twenty-seven writings of the New Testament. Only in the AD 390s did any of the church councils approve the list, one at Hippo and one at Carthage. What this indicates is that the twenty-seven books in my New Testament are there because God's people wanted them there, and the "official" councils only approved them after the people had already accepted them. And why did the people approve them? These twenty-seven books were practical. They were functional. They were useful. And these books have stood the test of time.

I do not state this to deny inspiration. Of course, the authors of my books were inspired—by God! But I do not tell you how they were inspired, other than to say that their writings were "God-breathed." But what does this mean? One writer has listed and described eight different theories of how I was inspired. But I don't tell you how I was inspired. I do tell you why! I was inspired so believers like you would be "equipped for every good work." You can find this phrase in 2 Timothy 3:17. See, I told you adding chapters and verses is a good idea. In other words, my authors were inspired by God for a practical reason. There was, and is, work to be done. I tell the people of God, including you, how to do it!

I am the Bible. I contain so many diverse types of literature: There is legal material (in Exodus, the Ten Commandments and the covenant code; in Deuteronomy, a repeat of the Ten Commandments); history (the Former Prophets; the Chronicler's History; information throughout the Law; the Latter Prophets; even the poetical literature); prophecy (the Former Prophets; the Latter Prophets; in much of the historical material); wisdom (Proverbs; some of the Psalms; Job; Ecclesiastes); poetry and liturgy (Psalms; some of the Proverbs; the Song of Solomon; Lamentations; some of the prophetic material); gospel (Matthew; Mark; Luke; John), church history (Acts); epistles (Paul's letters; the General Epistles), and apocalyptic literature (parts of Daniel and Zechariah; Revelation). As you can see, there are so many different ways to proclaim my message. And when it comes to interpreting my message, knowing the kind of literature you are reading is so vitally important.

I am the Bible. I was written originally in three different languages. Most of my old writings were in Hebrew, but some included Aramaic (parts of Daniel and Ezra and one verse in Jeremiah). Aramaic was the language used in Palestine by the Jews during the time of Jesus.

My newest books were written in *koine* Greek, the language of the common people. How appropriate! In fact, my Old Testament was translated into Greek a few centuries before Christ appeared. It was called the Septuagint, which means the "Seventy." The tradition was that seventy or seventy-two Jewish scholars, separate from one another, came up with identical translations from Hebrew into Greek during a seventy-day period. Of course, this was just a tradition, but the importance of the Septuagint cannot be overemphasized. Importantly, a number of books were added and were called the Apocrypha. This canon list was based upon what is called the "Alexandrian canon." Later, these books would be included in the Catholic canon, but rejected by the Protestant tradition in the sixteenth century.

Back to the Greek language. Greek was the universal language of the Roman Empire. It was used everywhere. My message could be read or proclaimed throughout the Roman world—and it was! God's timing was so good!

But since then I have been translated into many languages. In fact, I have been translated in my entirety into 698 different languages. My New Testament can be read in an additional 1,548 different languages. And at least one of my books can be found in another 1,138 languages. In other words, in whole or in part, I have been translated into 3,384 languages.[2] And this number keeps growing.

Now, let me ask you this: Aren't you glad you can read me in English? I'll bet most of you here today have let your Hebrew and Greek slip just a little.

Getting into English was not easy. John Wycliffe, the "morning star" of the Reformation, led in my being translated into English in the fourteenth century. But the printing press had not been invented at this time, so copies had to be made by hand. It was not until the mid-fifteenth century when I could finally be mass produced. And what was Wycliffe's reward? His bones were dug up about forty years after his death, burned, and the ashes were cast into a nearby stream called the Swift.

Even after the invention of the printing press, getting me translated into English was not easy. William Tyndale, the "Father of the English Bible," was burned at the stake by orders of Henry VIII for translating my New Testament into English. But Tyndale would not yield on his conviction that everyone should read the Scriptures in his or her own tongue.

But then other Bibles in English began to appear: the Coverdale Bible (the first complete printed Bible in English); the Thomas Matthew Bible; the Great Bible (it was called the Great Bible because it had great big pages); the Geneva Bible (the Bible of Shakespeare and the Pilgrim Fathers), which was translated by William Whittingham, an exile in Geneva during the reign of Queen Mary, and the brother-in-law of John Calvin; and the Bishop's Bible.

Then along came the King James Version in 1611. This means this translation turned four hundred years old in 2011! My, what a great history it has had; what a great work it has done for the cause of God's kingdom. It was the Bible of the English-speaking people for over three hundred years! It was revised later in several versions—the Revised Version (1885); the American Standard Version (1901); the Revised Standard Version (1952); the New American Standard Bible (1971); the New King James Version (1982); the New Revised Standard Version (1989). One could get confused with all the "alphabet" versions: the KJV; the ASV; the RSV; the NEB; the NASB; the NIV (1978); the NKJV; the REB (1987); and the NRSV. One of these days, one of the TV evangelists will announce they now have a video version of the Bible, and of course, they will call it the TVV!

And what about the Phillips translation, the Amplified Bible, the Moffat translation, the Living Bible, the Jerusalem Bible, and on and on? In the words of the old TV game show, "Will the real *biblos* please stand up?" Well, let me ask you, through which one or ones of these translations does God's message come to you when you read me? Maybe, if your hearts and minds are open, then God can use most or all of them in his work.

I am the Bible. I have a long history. I have been attacked and analyzed. I have been burned and banned. I have been criticized, condemned, and cursed. I have been laughed at and loathed. I've been ridiculed and ranted against. But I am still around. Where are my critics of days gone by? They are dead and gone. I live on. And I shall outlive my contemporary critics as well. As long as people like you read me, study me, interpret me, and apply me, I shall survive.

But what grieves me the most are not the attacks from my enemies. No, it is the divisiveness over me among my friends. I have become a source of debate between my supporters which has become so hostile, at times I wonder if any of them have actually read me? Oh, they surely have. But what kind of witness do they give to God when they haven't understood my message? God's people continue to argue with each other over me. They defend me with a viciousness which is frightening.

But when did I ever ask man to defend me? When did I ever need man to defend me? That's saying too much for man—and too little for me. I didn't become the world's number one best seller (which I am) because man defended me, but because my message is true and relevant, and because the lives of people who read me are changed. What I am saying is I grieve much more over the immaturity of my supporters than the assaults of my enemies.

And while I am at it, let me mention the current debate over me, a debate which has been around for many years. Followers argue over whether I am inerrant, infallible, reliable, or authoritative, and so on. If you listen carefully, you'll hear that the real issue is over my original manuscripts, or as the scholars call them, the "original autographs"—not over the translation you have. The question posed is, "What do you believe about me, the Bible, as I was originally written?" Let me tell you the true view about my originals, the view that can be absolutely proven based upon the current evidence: My original manuscripts are missing! You don't have them. You will probably never have them. And most of you, possibly all of you, could not read them if you did have them.

So, as far as I am concerned, the primary issue is, what are you going to do with what you have, not what you don't have? Haven't I always been good enough as I am?

But despite all the polemic and all the debate, I continue to be the spiritual catalyst which leads to changed lives! I was the source of study and mediation by the monks in the monasteries, whose faithfulness in making handwritten copies of me brought me through the darkness of the Middle Ages. I was the textbook for the Reformation, the authority and guide for Martin Luther, Huldrech Zwingli, John Calvin, the Anabaptists, the Puritans, and other reformers and reforming groups. There would have been no Great Awakening in the middle colonies, no Evangelical Revival led by John Wesley in England, no Second Awakening on the American frontier, no message for the English Baptist William Carey to take to India at the beginning of the modern missionary movement, and no cry for justice by Martin Luther King, Jr. in the twentieth century without me.

I am the Bible. And I continue to speak to the needs of people today. You can find me being taught in thousands of Sunday school and church classes and proclaimed from countless pulpits every Sunday. I am the daily subject of study in homes, colleges, and seminaries. I am the service manual for believers, pastors, evangelists, missionaries, and Christian workers everywhere.

My power to change lives and the world has never diminished. I am just as relevant today as I was when I was written. People are still separated from God and need redemption. The injustice attacked by the prophets still exists in your world today. The hungry still need to be fed; the thirsty still need water; the poor are still with you, needing clothing and shelter; and the sick and the imprisoned still need to be visited. Brotherly love continues to be a worthy goal in a world threatened by nuclear war, an environmental holocaust, or even artificial intelligence. No, my teachings have never been outdated.

My message continues to reach down into the souls of ordinary and extraordinary people and touch their lives. Men, women, and children; the rich and the poor; kings and commoners; princes and paupers; white, red, black, yellow and brown, and now many combinations thereof; in churches large and churches small, in all kinds of places throughout the earth, people still find in me a source of strength for their weaknesses, a guidepost when they need direction, and a model by which to live.

I am the Bible. But I do not point my readers and my students to myself. I point you to God, so you may know who God is. I point you to yourselves, so you may know who you are. And I point you to the world, where you may find your place of ministry and service.

But I must be read to be understood. I must be studied to be comprehended. I must be interpreted and applied to be relevant and meaningful in your world today!

I am worth nothing if I am the number one best seller of all time but become nothing more than a religious symbol that gathers dust on your shelves.

The words "Holy Bible" in gold printed on an expensive leather cover mean nothing if my pages are not worn from use by you.

I despise being defended in principle but ignored in practice.

I sense hypocrisy when believers call themselves the "people of the Book" but can't speak a clear and consistent word about what I say.

I feel abused when people pick and choose my verses to prove a distorted opinion, while failing to comprehend my total message.

Above all, I want to cry out "heresy" when people worship me instead of the living God toward whom I point. I never want to become a graven image. My only ambition is to be the book which points pilgrims like you to God.

And what do I want from you? I want you to read me, not just own me. I want you to love me because you have found the love of God through my pages. And I want you to keep on studying me. I have so much in me I want to share with you. I want you to develop your tools to properly interpret me. I want you to apply me to the way you live.

If you follow my teachings, you will find love in a world filled with hate. You will find peace amidst the anxieties of your day. You will find a mission, a service, and a purpose for living. Above all you will find God, who comes anew to you through me.

I am the Bible! I am a practical book that is different from any other book you will ever read. Read my pages and you will find that I already know who you are. What I want is for you to get to know me! If you do, you will become a better person. This world will become a better place. And the purpose of my existence will be fulfilled. Beginning right now, pledge yourself anew to read me, study me, and apply me. After all, I am the Bible. I am the Book!

MONOLOGUE 2: I AM JOHN MARK AND I WROTE THE FIRST GOSPEL

TEXTS:

Mark 1:1 – The beginning of the good news about Jesus the Messiah, the Son of God.

Acts 15:36-39 – Some time later Paul said to Barnabas, "Let us go back and visit the believers in all the towns where we preached the word of the Lord and see how they are doing." Barnabas wanted to take John, also called Mark, with them, but Paul did not think it wise to take him, because he had deserted them in Pamphylia and had not continued with them in the work. They had a major disagreement that they parted company. Barnabas took Mark and sailed for Cyprus.

1 Peter 5:13 – She who is in Babylon, chosen together with you, sends you her greetings, and so does my son Mark.

INTRODUCTION:

During the reign of Emperor Constantine in AD 325, Eusebius, bishop of Caesarea, completed his *Ecclesiastical History*, which traced the beginnings of Christianity up to the Council of Nicaea, the first general council of Christianity. Eusebius is considered to be the "Father of Church History." In *Ecclesiastical History*, he collected and included numerous documents from the church that otherwise would have been lost to history.

Because of the efforts of Eusebius, we are fortunate to have a written record of the first testimony related to the written Gospels. He recorded the testimony of Papias, the Bishop of Hierapolis in the early second century AD. Eusebius documented Papias as stating, "Mark, having become the interpreter of Peter, wrote down accurately, though not in order, whatsoever he remembered of the things said or done by Christ. For he neither heard the Lord nor followed him, but afterward, as I said, he followed Peter, who adapted his teaching to the needs of his hearers, but with no intention of giving a connected account of the Lord's discourses, so that Mark committed no error while he thus wrote some things as he remembered them. For he was careful of one thing, not to omit any of the things which he had heard, and not to state any of them falsely."[3]

This monologue accepts the testimony of Papias that Mark used the preaching of Peter in comprising his Gospel. It also assumes that Mark was the author of the first Gospel to be written, based upon the position prevalent among scholars that the authors of Matthew and Luke had access to and used the Gospel of Mark as a guide in writing their own Gospels. More importantly, it addresses the important question, "How was Mark qualified to write the first Gospel in the New Testament?"

Estimates of the date of the writing of Mark's Gospel range from around AD 50 to AD 70. My own interpretation would place the time around AD 65, give or take a few years, although this is a minority interpretation. Christianity had spread throughout the Roman Empire. The church had grown significantly and especially through gentile converts. The eyewitnesses to the life, ministry, and teachings of Jesus were dying off, either by natural causes or by execution. For example, according to tradition Peter and Paul were either nearing execution under Emperor Nero or had already been executed. Furthermore, Jesus had not returned, which many in the early church had expected.

Beginning in the middle of the first century AD, Paul was writing letters to individuals and churches. But someone needed to record a written testimony of God's revelation in Jesus that would preserve the witness of those who saw and heard Jesus. This testimony was also needed in order to teach the numerous converts to the faith, and if needed, for the ages to come.

So the question to be answered today is, "Just who was qualified to write a 'Gospel of Jesus Christ?'" Who had the knowledge, the experience, and the understanding of the story, along with the recognition of the need for such a written work? Who had the connections with the early leaders of the church that would lend credibility to his writing and give it the needed authority? The answer lies in the personal experience of John Mark. He was raised by a dedicated, influential Christian mother. He was taught and nurtured by some of the most influential personalities in the early church. His mentors included his uncle Barnabas, the apostle Paul, and the apostle Peter. Additionally, he most certainly would have conversed with other apostles and disciples in the early church in Jerusalem.

Furthermore, Mark apparently played a small part of the story of Jesus. Evidence points to Mark's presence during the last week of Jesus's life leading up to his arrest, crucifixion, and resurrection: Only in Mark's Gospel do we find the story of a young man in the garden of Gethsemane fleeing from the guards into the night (Mark 14:51-2). He later traveled with Barnabas and Saul for at least a part of their first missionary journey. He teamed with his uncle again on a second journey, and in fact was a source of conflict between Barnabas and Paul as they contemplated this journey. Later Mark united with Peter in doing mission work and heard the apostle's many stories about the life and teachings of Jesus. He served as the amanuensis or secretary of Peter, which surely refined his early writing skills and prepared him to be the author of the first written Gospel.

So, as we seek to answer the question, "How did we get the first written Gospel?" we can affirm it was not an accident but the result of many influences upon Mark. As we examine the contributions of those who influenced Mark, we should be reminded that we too have had numerous influences in our personal lives, and all of the important things we do are built upon the foundation of these influences. We should also be reminded that we influence people as we encounter them in our lives, and that we can and do make a difference—for good or for bad—in what they become, whether they be family, friends, or even total strangers. So, on this day, who better to tell us the story of how we came to have the first Gospel than John Mark himself. Listen to him attentively as he recalls his journey.

MONOLOGUE: I AM JOHN MARK AND I WROTE THE FIRST GOSPEL

Greetings and thanks for coming today. My name is Mark, or John Mark. I am really pleased to be with you. I am here simply to share with you my story about how I came to write the first Gospel of the four that would appear in the New Testament. To me, without question this is the most important contribution I will make in my life. So, stay with me as I narrate the story of all those who influenced me during my journey, and who deserve credit for my written testimony of the life of Jesus.

I grew up in Palestine, raised by a single, loving mother. My mother Mary became an early follower of Jesus, a carpenter from Nazareth, who was also considered a rabbi and a prophet by many. I too would become one of those followers. Mother ensured that I received a good education. I attended a rabbi's school in a synagogue, which was the primary source of education in the Jewish tradition, especially in the study of the Law and the Prophets. My education enhanced my skills at reading and writing, which were essential in preparing me to take on the significant task of writing the first Gospel.

Mother also instilled in me an inquiring attitude. She set an example as a dedicated and sharing Christian who opened her home to the early followers of Jesus. She showed courage as a woman in a world in which women were usually fifth and sixth class citizens. Her self-confidence provided a good foundation from which she became a follower of Jesus. From this perspective, she provided an influential and positive model that encouraged me to have confidence in myself and what I could do. She encouraged me to broaden my understanding and to openly encounter those who came from different backgrounds, and she gave me the freedom and support to travel to new places and observe different cultures. Her influence can be seen in my universal awareness of both Jewish and gentile believers.

Our home became an important gathering place in Jerusalem for Jesus and his followers. As a young lad, I was able to listen to Jesus and his disciples discuss important issues related to religion and faith. It was obvious to me Jesus was not an ordinary teacher; he had wisdom and insight and he displayed love and compassion for those in need of guidance. I can see why so many were attracted to his teachings and his example. I certainly was.

Near the end of his ministry, he came into conflict with the religious leaders in Jerusalem, the center of the Jewish faith. Horrifically, this would result in his crucifixion. On the night he was arrested I had sneaked out of my house with only a linen sheet wrapped around me. I had already gone to bed, but I knew something important was going on. I could just feel it. And I wanted to be a part of whatever happened. I discovered that Jesus had gathered his disciples together for a last special meal. I thought it was the Passover meal, but it was different.

After the meal they went to the garden of Gethsemane, where Jesus alone went deeper into the garden to pray. I was hanging around with the apostles, staying out of the way. All of a sudden, guards of the high priest appeared with swords and clubs. Total chaos broke loose. One of the followers of Jesus even cut an ear off one of the guards. People started fleeing. So did I. A guard reached out and tried to grab me but ended up ripping off my bed sheet. I ran off naked, streaking into the night, as your generation might say. I guess I am the first "streaker" in the New Testament. You probably won't find this story included in any other Gospels, which are sure to be written. But it is my way of subtly saying "Hey, I was there. I saw it all take place."

Of course, you all know what happened. Jesus was arrested and tried before several individuals and groups. Under Pontius Pilate, the Roman governor, he was sentenced to die. He was crucified and hastily buried before the Sabbath began. His body was claimed by Joseph of Arimathea, a member of the Sanhedrin, who provided a newly cut tomb. We all thought this was the end of the story of a very good man who suffered a tragic death. Boy, were we wrong. On Sunday morning everything changed. But I don't need to tell you the story. You already know it.

Let me get back to my story. Mother had a brother. He was Joseph, a member of the tribe of Levi and a businessman. His home was on the island of Cyprus, making him a Jew of the diaspora, the Jews dispersed throughout the Roman Empire. Because of this he was in frequent contact with gentiles. He felt comfortable with them. I learned this skill when I worked with him later on.

Uncle Joseph had a nickname, "Barnabas," which means "Son of Encouragement." No one could be more appropriately characterized, as you will soon understand. I think he became a follower of Jesus because of Mother. At least he met followers of Jesus in our house. Uncle Barnabas was always open to new ideas, and apparently the idea that Jesus was the long-expected Messiah resonated with him. He quickly became a devoted follower of Jesus and a leader in the movement.

He acted out of faithfulness to Jesus and to the fellowship in Jerusalem. Not long after Pentecost, he saw many followers of Jesus who were hungry and poor in Jerusalem. He was well-to-do, so he sold a piece of property in the city and gave the money to the apostles to distribute to the needy.

Barnabas had many laudable qualities. Above all else, he saw the good in people, especially in those whom others would find a way to look down upon. But not my Uncle Barnabas. He saw the potential in their lives. He encouraged them to recognize who they were and what they could do. He was courageous and always willing to take a chance on so many, myself included. Later, he would become a leader in a church at Antioch. He had been sent there by the leaders in Jerusalem to proclaim the faith. I am certain he led those at Antioch to accept both Jews and gentiles into the new work on an equal basis. Being a Hellenistic Jew, he worked easily with gentiles and, as I said, he always seemed to see the good in people. The church at Antioch paved the way for reaching out with the message about Jesus not only to Jews but also to gentiles.

One superb example was following the conversion of Saul. You know the story: how Saul, a Roman citizen from Tarsus and a dedicated student of the Jewish Law, became an aggressive persecutor of followers of Jesus. He had watched Stephen being stoned because of his witness for Jesus. It probably didn't help Stephen's case when he called past religious leaders "killers of the prophets." A pronouncement like this won't make you many friends.

Saul was offended that this collection of commoners, fishermen, and tax collectors claimed to have had a revelation from God. As an ardent defender of the Jewish Law, he found this claim by these "Christians" to be absurd. He needed no revelation beyond the Law, and he set out to prove it by persecuting believers.

He was so successful in Jerusalem in arresting believers of Jesus and bringing them before the religious authorities that he sought and received permission to go to Damascus and arrest Jesus's followers there. However, something happened on the road to Damascus that radically reversed his life. He was confronted by a blinding light and a voice asking why Saul was persecuting him. He took it to be a revelation from Jesus, did a 180-degree turn in his life, and went into Damascus a changed man.

Ananias, a believer in Jesus, took him under his wing and taught him about our Lord. Saul became an ardent preacher of faith in Jesus. In fact, Saul the persecutor became Saul the persecuted. He wound up being lowered over the city wall in a basket in order to escape. I suppose your generation will conclude that Saul became the first basket case in the early church.

But let me continue with my story. Saul eventually made his way to the church in Jerusalem, where a big celebration was held for him. If you believe this, then I have some prime farmland in the Negev desert to sell you. The leaders of the church were initially suspicious of Saul, and rightly so. After all, he was the grand inquisitor of the early believers; why should he be believed with his "dramatic conversion" story?

But Uncle Barnabas, who happened to be visiting the city, talked with Saul and affirmed him. The leaders trusted Barnabas and decided to take a chance on Saul. What an important decision this was for the advancement of Christianity! I told you Uncle Barnabas looked for the good in people, didn't I? Later he sought out and invited Saul to join him in his work in Antioch. About a year later, when a famine was devastating the area, Barnabas and Saul took a collection from the Antioch church to the impoverished Christians in Judaea. When they returned to Antioch, they took me along.

I was pretty excited and ready to set out on a new adventure. Besides, I was young and wanted to see new things, experience a wider world, and establish my own identity. Uncle Barnabas saw my potential. With his being like a father figure to me and my mother trusting him a lot, she encouraged me to go with them to Antioch.

I also wanted to learn more about Jesus, and who better to teach me than my uncle? He filled in a lot of gaps in my knowledge. Although he wasn't an apostle, he was close friends with so many of them. He had heard their stories and shared those stories with me. He told me about Jesus's teachings and his mighty deeds, his love and care for those neglected by society, and his courage in standing up for the down-and-out and those rejected by traditional religious leadership. Above all, my uncle lived out the example Jesus provided for all of his followers, and he was a dedicated practitioner and preacher of this good news from God in Jesus.

I learned so much from what he said, what he did, and how he cared for me as his nephew. But I also learned a lot from Saul. He and my uncle were so different. My uncle saw the good in people. Saul...well, you got one chance with him. I should know. I'll tell you that story in a few minutes.

When the Antioch church felt led by the Spirit to send out a missionary party to take the gospel of Jesus to new places, they chose Barnabas and Saul. My uncle invited me to go along. What a learning experience that would be. We took a ship to Cyprus, which you remember is where Uncle Barnabas lived. Oh, that trip was a fun. We travelled to so many places on the island. And I continued to learn so much from my uncle and Saul.

Saul was a remarkable thinker. He had spent about three years in the desert contemplating what had happened to him on the road to Damascus, and what it meant in relation to the Law and God's revelation in Jesus. He was not "ashamed of the gospel," that is for sure. He became an ardent defender of justification by faith alone and the freedom Jesus brings to the believer.

Saul would be the one who recognized the importance of taking the gospel directly to the gentiles. What a major step this was! In terms of understanding the universal nature of the Christian message, he contributed more than any other believer, and he was willing to face persecution in order to proclaim his message. I really came to appreciate the importance of sharing the Christian faith to all people from both Saul and my uncle. Furthermore, Saul's letter writing gave me the incentive to preserve in writing the message of and about Jesus. He set an example to make sure my message was clear and rational.

After we crossed the Great Sea and reached Perga in Pamphlia, I wanted to go home. I was getting homesick. I missed my mother and I missed Jerusalem. I was also wondering about what lay before us. Could it be dangerous? For Saul and my uncle, it truly was, I found out later on. I might also point out that Saul began to be referred to as Paul from here on. Paul was the Roman way of saying Saul, as I understand it, and Paul was a Roman citizen. It was at this stage of our journey when he began to preach directly to the gentiles.

He also became the leader of the mission party as they moved into Asia Minor. My uncle was not a jealous person and didn't mind the change. He recognized Paul as an outstanding leader and visionary, and he accepted his new role in their work together. Even as I went back home, I realized how life-changing this new experience had been for me. Later, I would truly realize its importance as I put the good news of Jesus into writing.

After reporting to the leaders of the church in Jerusalem about their missionary success, especially among the gentiles, Paul and Barnabas decided to head out on a second missionary journey. Barnabas wanted to take me along again, and I was ready to go. But like I said, Paul gave me one chance and I had blown it. So I went with my uncle back to Cyprus, which was fine with me. Paul took Silas instead, and they visited the churches in Asia Minor. Then they went to Macedonia, crossing the Aegean Sea at Troas. Before reaching Troas, they had picked up Timothy, a half Jewish, half gentile young man at Lystra. While they were at Troas, a physician named Luke joined them briefly on their way to Philippi. Paul's team now was taking the gospel into Europe. Luke, as I understand later in my life, would also begin to write a

Gospel narrative. I also heard that he was preparing an account of the early church that will record how the gospel was taken from Jerusalem all the way to Rome.

Uncle Barnabas continued to teach me, and I shall always cherish the memories of my missionary travels with him and be grateful for all he taught me. But I eventually wound up being attached to Peter. I really liked Peter. He was bold and boisterous. His heart, if not always his mind, was in the right place. He was both enthusiastic and humble. He was a man of courage and conviction. He spent time under arrest and in prison. He was a preacher much more than a philosopher. And he was a missionary as well, although he didn't become as well-known in this role as Paul did. In the end he was also willing to live and die for the gospel—and he did.

Peter did missionary work in several provinces in Asia Minor. As I told you, I was his amanuensis. The writing skills I learned from my mother really paid off. Peter engaged in a lot of correspondence with his friends in Judea, Galilee, and well, everywhere he traveled. I learned even more about Jesus and the work of the church as I transcribed and answered his correspondence.

I also recognized the importance of preserving his witness to Jesus. When he preached, he told all these wonderful stories of his time with Jesus. He told of Jesus's compassion for people, of his miraculous deeds in response to the faith of common, ordinary people, and of his conflicts with authorities. He spoke of Jesus's marvelous teachings, of his death, and of his resurrection. Peter was as close to Jesus as any of the apostles. The people loved to hear his personal stories about Jesus, which he told with such passion.

I began taking copious notes. I wrote down all I heard. I was careful to be accurate because I realized how important Peter's testimony might be. Being a fisherman, his writing skills were limited. This is actually one of the reasons he enlisted me as his secretary. It was one of the most important tasks I could have had considering the nature of the times. It was time for the good news of Jesus to be written down, and I was the one with the skills, the experience, and the opportunity to do it.

Picture this with me. Several decades had passed since the ministry of Jesus. Many expected that he would return quickly, so there was no need for a written gospel. Jesus never wrote down anything we know of. We only had those who were eyewitnesses of his teachings, his ministry, and his mighty deeds who could tell these fascinating stories. But many of these had died, some because of persecution, some from natural causes. Soon there would be no one who could say, "I remember Jesus when..." and then share personal memories. The stories were becoming secondhand accounts, losing some of their freshness, and possibly even becoming distorted.

Besides, many new converts were coming into the church, especially gentiles. Who would teach them; who would tell them about Jesus and all he said and did? I had the unique opportunity of recording all of these marvelous stories which would last through the generations. I knew several important leaders intimately: my mother, my uncle, and Paul. But most importantly, I had been fortunate enough to travel extensively with Peter and listen to his colorful stories about Jesus. As I began to write them down, I tried to put them into some kind of order. I felt as qualified as anyone to preserve the witness and testimony of Peter and the many other close followers of Jesus. I knew most of the apostles. I had listened to them tell their respective stories. I have no doubt I was the person to carry out the monumental task of being the first to write down the good news of Jesus.

And the time was crucial. Rome was now persecuting Christians. Emperor Nero needed a scapegoat for the burning of a major part of Rome. Suspicions were that he had started the fire in order to rebuild the city in a glorious manner that would bring praise to him. As a diversion he began to persecute Christians. Some of them, after all, had spoken of a fiery end to the age. They were prime suspects, even though Roman historians absolved them of any blame.

Peter had been arrested in Rome and would soon be executed. His witness had to be preserved. And again, I was the one to do it. Paul was also in trouble and had appealed to Rome to have his case heard by Caesar. He was a Roman citizen, and this was his right. But it also was dangerous, and he too was risking his life. As I saw it, my written Gospel could complement his letters to Christians and churches, which were being copied and circulated extensively.

So, I set out to complete my writing in the form of an account of the good news, or the "gospel," of Jesus. And I did. The story of Jesus was now written down. Some of us began to copy my account by hand to share with churches throughout the empire. The witness of Peter and others was now preserved and it would not be lost. Now, nearly two millennia later, you are still reading this written witness of the good news in Jesus. You hear the stories of Jesus as told by those eyewitnesses, and especially by Peter. You can teach your children and friends, and you can help make disciples of Jesus based upon my written account. The fact that I was not an apostle adds credence to my account. The tradition connecting me with this book is founded upon solid ground, upon the merit of my book.

As you now know, Matthew and Luke also wrote Gospels. Matthew was concerned about the decline of Jewish Christianity in light of the growing influence of gentile Christianity. He emphasized Jesus's Jewish heritage by applying the wonderful Jewish titles to him. He compared the teachings of Jesus to Moses and the Law, and affirmed Jesus as the Messiah, or Christ. Luke was a gentile, His Gospel emphasized the universal nature of Christianity. He placed his gospel in a thoroughly Romanized world, which was important in witnessing to gentiles. In fact, he emphasized Jesus as the Savior of the whole world. I am sure that these two writers borrowed from my Gospel while writing their own. They also added collections of teachings of Jesus that were circulating, Finally they included their own special stories which contributed to the understanding of Jesus.

My own journey convinces me that when God needs something to be done, he calls a qualified person to do it. I listened, I learned, I studied, and I had the skills to write a Gospel account of Jesus. I was influenced and encouraged by others. But in the end, I realized what needed to be done, and concluded I was the one who could do it. So I wrote my Gospel.

Today, as you read my two-thousand-year-old Gospel, or more accurately, the gospel of Jesus, remember those who made a difference in your lives. Who are those people who have made a difference in who you are? Who caused you to radically change, or to reshape your understanding of people, the world, and the church? To whom do you owe a debt of gratitude when it comes to evaluating your understanding, your contributions to your world, and your faith? And don't forget to appreciate your personal journey and the continual shaping and reshaping of your faith.

Let me also remind you that who you are and who you may become will contribute to the next and following generations, whether you make the history books or not. I lived almost two thousand years ago, but the influence of my Gospel and the influence of those who touched my life are evident in the pages of this book which you continue to study and appreciate even today. And this influence is not about to diminish. Who would have predicted this could happen?

Your life will bear fruit in the lives of others. If you contribute to someone becoming a better person, who helps those around him or her and who influences the next generation, then the cycle of your lives will come full circle. Who knows what unnamed person years from now will be a better person and make a greater contribution simply because you made a difference in someone's life, and that person made a difference for someone else, and that person made a difference, and so on and so on.

So, in conclusion, how my Gospel came to be written is a story that has a lot more to it than you might realize. Furthermore, my story should remind you of the importance of your own stories, and of the influences upon your lives, and of the influence of your lives. You all are important; may you be reminded of that on this day! My friends, this will indeed be good news!

MONOLOGUE 3: THE PRODIGAL SON

TEXT:

Luke 15:11-32 – Jesus continued: "There was a man who had two sons. The younger one said to his father, 'Father, give me my share of the estate.' So he divided his property between them.

"Not long after that, the younger son got together all he had, set off for a distant country and there squandered his wealth in wild living. After he had spent everything, there was a severe famine in that whole country, and he began to be in need. So he went and hired himself out to a citizen of that country, who sent him to his fields to feed pigs. He longed to fill his stomach with the pods that the pigs were eating, but no one gave him anything.

"When he came to his senses, he said, 'How many of my father's hired servants have food to spare, and here I am starving to death! I will set out and go back to my father and say to him: 'Father, I have sinned against heaven and against you. I am no longer worthy to be called your son; make me like one of your hired servants.' So he got up and went to his father.

"But while he was still a long way off, his father saw him and was filled with compassion for him; he ran to his son, threw his arms around him and kissed him.

"The son said to him, 'Father, I have sinned against heaven and against you. I am no longer worthy to be called your son.'

"But the father said to his servants, 'Quick! Bring the best robe and put it on him. Put a ring on his finger and sandals on his feet. Bring the fattened calf and kill it. Let's have a feast and celebrate.

For this son of mine was dead and is alive again; he was lost and is found.' So they began to celebrate.

"Meanwhile, the older son was in the field. When he came near the house, he heard music and dancing. So he called one of the servants and asked him what was going on. 'Your brother has come,' he replied, 'and your father has killed the fattened calf because he has him back safe and sound.'

"The older brother became angry and refused to go in. So his father went out and pleaded with him. But he answered his father, 'Look! All these years I've been slaving for you and never disobeyed your orders. Yet you never gave me even a young goat so I could celebrate with my friends. But when this son of yours who has squandered your property with prostitutes comes home, you kill the fattened calf for him!'

"'My son,' the father said, 'you are always with me, and everything I have is yours. But we had to celebrate and be glad, because this brother of yours was dead and is alive again; he was lost and is found.'"

INTRODUCTION:

As a retired professor of religion, I like to point out that Jesus was known more for being a teacher than a preacher. He used numerous teaching techniques to proclaim his message, including similes, hyperbole, poetry, etc. But his most well-known technique was the parable. A parable is a story or teaching device that always seems to have in mind the question, to what can this be compared? The use of parables is found in most cultures and the art of storytelling is a great gift. Jesus was a master at teaching with parables, and there are more than fifty found in the Synoptic Gospels alone.

Collections of parables: A parable does not have to be a true story, but it contains truth in the form of a short story. Several well-known parables are found in Matthew 13, including the parable of the sower, the wheat and the tares, the mustard seed, the leaven, the hidden treasure, the pearl of great price, and the fisherman's net. In Luke 15 there are three famous parables: the parables of the lost sheep, the lost coin, and the lost son. Today we are going to look at the parable of the lost son, which is better known as the parable of the prodigal son. I will present this story through the eyes of that son, using another teaching device known as the monologue. Next week the older brother will show up to tell his side of the story. I give to you, the Prodigal Son.

MONOLOGUE OF THE PRODIGAL SON

Well, good morning! Wow, here I am, back home in the comfort of my family and friends. Hey, it's good to be back home again, sleeping in my own bed, basking in the glow of a nice party with my friends. Wow, did those steaks taste great!! This is a lot different than the situation I found myself in just a few weeks ago, and to be honest with you, it's not exactly what I expected. So, do you want to know what I'm talking about? Well, most of you have already heard my story but let me take a few minutes and retell it from my perspective.

For starters I am the younger of two sons in a world that certainly favors being firstborn. For example, the firstborn becomes the leader of the family, not because he has done anything to deserve it but simply because he happened to be born first. Those of us "untimely born" don't have the opportunity to display our talents and leadership skills. We are simply left out when it comes to succeeding our fathers as head of the house. And not only this, but the firstborn gets a double portion of the inheritance when my father's estate "matures." Let me ask you, what did my older brother ever do to deserve a double share of everything? Not much. Quite simply, he was born before me. Big deal! So what?

I'll tell you this: my older brother is really difficult to get along with. He thinks he is in charge around here and I am just another servant. He is so bossy, so pushy. He acts like *he* owns this place, not my father. I don't know why my father puts up with him, but he does.

Speaking of my father, he really is a good person, and certainly a good father. However, he is too tolerant of my arrogant brother. But he does seem to genuinely appreciate all he does, and he has always seemed to accept and understand me. I am sure I have caused him to lose sleep at night. But what son hasn't? Well, maybe my dull and boring older brother, but he is the exception.

So, what was I to do? There was no future here for me, unless I wanted to be a puppet in the hands of my older brother. I wanted some adventure; I wanted to see the world; I wanted to do things my way; I wanted to show that I am worth something, I have dreams and ideas, and I can succeed out there without my older brother always checking up on me.

This is why I did what I did not too long ago. I decided to go to my father and demand—no, *ask*—for my share of the inheritance. Of course, I only get a third of the inheritance. My brother gets two-thirds, you know. Still, I'll take what I can get, and I might as well get it now. Our culture allows this, you know. So, I decided to set out on my own and prove to my father and brother—and to myself—that I could make my own way without looking over my shoulder to see if my brother was watching. He always seems to be watching everything I do.

So, I took my inheritance, walked out the door, marched down the road, shoulders held high, and set out to discover my future. Boy, that felt good! Man, was I excited! I wanted to get as far away from that place as I could...and away from my brother, of course. I headed for a distant place I had heard about—one which had never heard of me, I might add.

It didn't take me too many days to arrive at my destination. Nice city, wide open, lots of opportunities for a young man out to show the world what he is made of. Of course I made lots and lots of new friends. I'm a really likable guy, and they seemed to like a person who had a sense of freedom and adventure, a dreamer and a doer. That's me! They also seemed to like the fact that I had quite a bit of money to spread around and I was generous with my resources. Wouldn't you like me? Of course you would.

Boy, did I have a good time. New friends. No rules. Party into the night. No older brother checking up on me. It doesn't get any better than that. Or at least it didn't until the money ran out. For some reason, my new friends also disappeared about the same time the money disappeared. I don't know where they went. But they sure left in a hurry!

But that was OK. I was tired of all the parties and it was time for me to get to work and show the world what a great success I was going to be. But boy, was my timing bad! The problem was, there was a famine in the land. Money and work were scarce. I could find no job. I was destitute, people. I looked and looked and looked for work. I was out of money, out of friends, and out of luck. The one who really cared for me, my father, was a long way off. Even my older brother would have looked pretty good right then. Did I really just say that? I must have been hallucinating!

Finally, I found a job, the only one around. It wasn't much but I was desperate. I found a job feeding swine. For a young Jewish lad, it doesn't get much lower than that. It would have been humiliating if I hadn't been so broke—and so hungry. The pigs' food was the pods of carob trees, the stuff the poorest people and farm animals eat. Pride disappears when you are hungry. I found myself eating the carob tree pods.

I was at the lowest point in my life. Desperate people sometimes take desperate measures. In my case, I had to take a realistic view of my situation, humble myself, and make one of the toughest decisions of my life. I "came to myself," that's a good way of putting it. I took a hard, honest look at where my decisions had landed me, and I didn't like what I saw one bit. But all of my problems were my own doing. I could not blame my situation on anyone else, not even my older brother.

I decided I would go home. Home may not be the best term. I had forfeited everything I had there. But I knew even the servants in my father's home had a much better life than I did. So I decided to go back and ask—actually beg—just to be a servant in my father's house. I had no right to anything else, and maybe not even that. But, as I told you, my father is a good man, and perhaps he might show a little mercy and let me work as a servant. This would be a lot better than feeding pigs and eating their food.

I could also just imagine my brother's reaction when I showed up. He wouldn't like my returning. No doubt he loved it when I left—except for me taking my inheritance. He would not hesitate to say to anyone who would listen, "See, I told you so." Big brothers are like that, you know. He would probably never let up in pointing out what a failure I was. But if that's what it takes, that's what it takes. He'd be right, but he would also be unable to show any mercy whatsoever. And I might add, my mistakes would not make him a better person, although he would try to plant that impression in the minds of others.

So, my decision was made. I set out toward home. I worked on my speech all the way back. I am sure many of you have done the same thing when facing a difficult situation, maybe even a confrontation. I planned to go right up to my father, head bowed, hat in hand, and tell him I had sinned against God and him. You know, disobedience to your parents is in a sense disobedience to God. I know enough of the commandments to understand this.

I decided to tell him I was no longer worthy to be called one of his sons—and I wasn't. I had denied every right to be considered a son of my father. I would simply ask—or as I said, beg—to be considered one of his hired hands. I went over and over my speech. I had plenty of time on the road home (or should I say the road back) to get it down just the way I wanted. I was embarrassed, but I was ready. I knew who I was and what I had to do. When you face yourself with complete honesty, you can find the courage to face anything before you. You can find the strength to be genuinely humble. And by this time, I was certainly humble.

And I will tell you this. It was a lot better to be Number Two at home than Number One in a pig pen. It would even be much better to be a servant in my father's house than Number One in a swine palace.

I was ready to face my past, ready to try and rebuild my future. I was still at a distance when I saw a familiar figure coming towards me. He was in a hurry. He looked really familiar. I quickly realized it was my father, who had seen me coming.

I got the impression he must have been looking for me, expecting me to return someday. He was genuinely glad to see me. He grabbed me, hugged me, and kissed me. I was not expecting this response. I quickly gave him my prepared speech. It was almost as though he didn't even hear me.

He immediately called out to a servant to quickly do three things. First, he told him to bring the best robe and put it on me. Then, he told him to put a ring on my finger. Finally, he told him to put sandals on my feet. Now, lest you think these are insignificant matters, they are not.

The robe signifies royalty. I was seen as a prominent member of my father's household, even though I no longer deserved it.

The ring was not just an ordinary ring. It was a signet ring, displaying the family crest. It symbolized authority. It was used to seal official documents. One would press the face of the ring into wax, then onto the document to affirm its validity. The ring on my finger symbolized that I was recognized as a true member of my father's family. I wasn't a servant. I was truly a son!

Finally, the sandals represented sonship. Sons wore sandals. Servants did not. By the robe, the ring, and the sandals, my father was saying I was his son! As wayward as I had been, as foolish as I had acted, my father still loved me and accepted me as his son.

And not only that! For my father my return was a cause for celebration. He planned a party, invited my friends and the neighbors, and prepared the fattened calf. It was an event fit for a king! I never felt so unworthy while at the same time so happy. It was good to be back home, surrounded by the love of my father and friends. In fact, my father saw me as a dead son who had come back to life.

As for my brother, well, I'll let him tell you his story at another time. I'm sure it will be most revealing and probably extremely boring

So, what are you to make of all of this? Maybe the answer lies in the teaching of a rabbi and a prophet I heard about during my "prodigal" stage of life. If I remember correctly, the guy was from Nazareth. He apparently wasn't like those legalistic teachers, the scribes and Pharisees. All they ever do is tell you what you can't do. Oh, this teacher recognized value in the law. But he understood something much deeper. He observed people, their needs, and their shortcomings. He called for people to love one another, to accept each other, and to work at growing in their relationships with their neighbors and even their enemies. This teacher really sounded radical, that's for sure. But what he said also made a lot of sense.

He also called upon us to grow in our relationship with God. You don't think much about God when you are living a wayward life like I was. But I was told that this teacher—I think his name was Jesus—taught us to pray to God like this: "Our Father who is in heaven." What an unique way of looking at God—as our father. Do you know what? After seeing how my father treated me upon my return, I like what the teacher said. My father had every reason to stop loving me, but he didn't. He could have thrown me out of his place, but he didn't. He knew who I was. He knew of my failures and shortcomings. He knew how weak I was.

But he opened his arms. He accepted me back home. He loved me. And he rejoiced when I returned home.

Is God like this? I think so. We fail him; we reject him; we disappoint him. But he is always ready to receive us back with open arms. I didn't have a long list of good deeds to defend myself. I hadn't kept the law. That certainly is easy to document; in fact, you could start at my failure to honor my father and mother and go from there.

All I could do was confess my failures, my shortcomings, and my mistakes. All I could do was say I was unworthy and ask to simply be a servant in my father's household. And all he did was love me, forgive me, and accept me fully and completely as his son. I still paid the consequences of my past. I had squandered my inheritance: there would be no more. But I could also rebuild my life, and I could draw upon my failures to become a better son. And in the eyes and the actions of my father, I was truly his son. And I am really glad to be able to say this!

I think the prophet from Nazareth was right on target. God is our father and we are his children. I am sure most of you listening to me understand exactly what I am saying. If not, think about my story and think about how God loves you as a son or a daughter. Hopefully, all of us will recognize that our journeys will make us more humble, make us more aware of a parent's love, and make us realize how fortunate we are to be able to call God "our Father."

EXTRA OPTIONS:

Invocation: Our God, this morning as we listen to the parable of Jesus about the wayward son, we are humbled by our shortcomings as your children. And once again, we are genuinely touched by the outpouring of your grace and forgiveness. We are not deserving of your compassion and acceptance. Yet, we depend upon them constantly.

On this day we find fellowship with you. We also find fellowship through worship with one another. As you accept us, help us to accept each other. As you forgive us, help us to forgive one another. As you demonstrate mercy to each of us, may we be merciful to one another, both in this place with these people and in our community with our friends and with strangers. As you are fatherly and motherly toward us, as the father was in receiving his prodigal son, and as the woman was in searching for the lost coin, encourage us to follow your example as well.

We are reminded that it was said of the Prodigal Son, he "came to himself." Help us to wake up to ourselves, and to you. Set us free from the illusion of trying to be perfect so we might be more fully human. Help us not to chase after an imaginary life, but to find satisfaction in our real lives. And turn us away from our self-rejection so we might see your arms open as you welcome us home. In the name of Jesus, the Son of the Father, we ask this prayer. Amen.

Benediction: Recite the Lord's Prayer, or say, "As the father came out to greet and welcome his son home, let us go forth to let our friends and neighbors know that they too are welcome as we worship our loving God together. Amen."

MONOLOGUE 4: A FATHER AND THE OLDER BROTHER

TEXT:
Luke 15:11 – Jesus continued: "There was a man who had two sons..." [Recount the story of the prodigal]

Luke 15:25-32 – "Now his older son was in the field, and when he came and approached the house, he heard music and dancing. And he summoned one of the servants and began inquiring what these things could be. And he said to him, 'Your brother has come, and your father has killed the fattened calf because he has received him back safe and sound.' But he became angry and was not willing to go in; and his father came out and began pleading with him. But he answered and said to his father, 'Look! For so many years I have been serving you and I have never neglected a command of yours; and yet you have never given me a young goat, so that I might celebrate with my friends; but when this son of yours came, who has devoured your wealth with prostitutes, you killed the fattened calf for him.' And he said to him, 'Son, you have always been with me, and all that is mine is yours. But we had to celebrate and rejoice, for this brother of yours was dead and has begun to live, and was lost and has been found.'"

INTRODUCTION:
Last week we looked at the story of the wayward son as seen through the eyes of the Prodigal, as he is called. I pointed out that Jesus was an outstanding teacher who effectively used the teaching technique of the parable, a word which means "to cast along-

side." I pointed out that a parable is a story that always seems to have in mind the question, to what can this be compared? Although not unique in terms of his use of parables, Jesus was a master of teaching with parables and there are more than fifty found in the Synoptic Gospels alone.

A number of parables are found in the Gospel of Luke. Luke has a special interest in the underdogs of society, including gentiles (or non-Jews), women, the physically challenged, children, and those rejected according to the standards of the Pharisees and Sadducees. Paralleling these thoughts, Luke, who is the only non-Jewish writer in the New Testament, emphasizes the universality of the good news.

In chapter 15 Luke records three famous parables: the lost sheep, the lost coin, and the lost son, all of which demonstrate the care God has for those who were rejected by Palestinian society and religion in the first century, and for those whom God seeks out to make beneficiaries of his love and concern.

This morning we are going to continue to examine the parable of a father and his two sons, which is better known collectively as the parable of the prodigal son. Perhaps we could call today's lesson the "parable of the older son." We will present this story primarily through the eyes of the older, loyal, hard-working son, who takes a legalistic approach to life. But first, having previously studied the younger, freedom-loving Prodigal Son, we should hear what the father of the two boys has to say.

MONOLOGUE OF THE OLDER SON AND A VISIT FROM THE FATHER

FATHER: Good morning! It's great to be here in your city. This city reminds me of the city where my younger son journeyed off to not long ago to engage in some rather frivolous living! (I hope you see the humor here.) That venture proved to be a real learning experience for my young man.

Here's a question for you. How many of you present today have children, especially sons? Being a parent is quite a challenge, no question about it. I have two sons. My oldest is a hard worker, disciplined, dedicated, dependable, and committed to clear and simple rules and regulations. He has few questions in life and he anticipates the day when, how shall I say this...when I am no longer around. He will assume leadership in our family!

My younger son, well, he is like most sons who are the youngest: adventuresome, free, living for the moment. In fact, I understand he showed up here recently and told you his story. I'll bet that was fascinating, and maybe even enlightening. He has always had a unique take on life and a colorful way with words. And I am sure it was obvious to you that he never lacks genuine enthusiasm. He is certainly optimistic, unlike his older brother who seems to find something negative to say no matter what the situation might be.

I love both of my sons, but sometimes...well, those of you who have more than one son, or maybe even more than one child, you know what I'm talking about.

So today, I have asked my oldest son to come and tell you his story so you can see things through his eyes. I believe in fair play and in allowing all sides to be heard. I can't say that about everyone! And I have learned it's not very wise of me to try and speak for either of my children.

Here comes my eldest now. I encourage you to listen carefully to what he has to say, even if you don't agree with him. He can present his views better than I can. So listen with me. He's almost here. And he won't have to worry about his younger brother. He will be along a little later, as soon as he wakes up!

ELDER SON: Good morning. And I must say, "Morning is good!" I love being out here working when the sun comes up. And I will keep working until the sun goes down. I do enjoy work. I find it most invigorating, don't you?

Let me tell you something right up front that I think is especially important for you to understand concerning my point of view. Everything I have, and will have, I will have earned, believe me. Early to bed, early to rise, this's my motto. Too bad my father's younger son doesn't see things my way. What a waste he is. He's in there sleeping while I'm out here slaving away. He makes me so angry, let me tell you. He is allergic to work. In fact, I don't even think he can spell "work." It's a four-letter word to him!

But that's not even the half of it. Here's what happened not too long ago. I know he has already told some of you his "interpretation" of these events. But you need to know the truth, what really happened, and what it all means. I might point out, it was all so disgusting that it just infuriates me when I think about it. But I suppose if I try really hard, I can talk about it without getting too upset.

For starters, I am the older of two sons in a world which does favor, I must admit, being firstborn. As firstborn, I am—or should I say will become—the leader of the family, but not simply because I happened to be born first. From the time I entered this world, or soon after, I have been working and training to take over from my father when the time comes—although you and I know that even now I am already carrying out most of the responsibilities while my father sits back and watches! I suppose he has earned his leisure, but I have spent years studying, watching, observing, and most of all doing! All my father's youngest has had to do is sit around daydreaming. His mind is always off somewhere else, leaving me to do the work! I know he is jealous of me. You can see it in his eyes. He imagines he could do things so much better than I. What a joke! He doesn't have a clue about how to run this place, or how hard it really is.

People think I have it made. Being the oldest, it's true I am next in line when it comes to leadership in our family—that is, when my father either becomes too old or passes on. At that time, when my father is no longer around, I am entitled to a double share of the family estate.

But I must repeat, I will have earned everything I receive when this day comes. Everything! I have always been obedient to my father (even when I think he is wrong! And boy, has he been wrong a lot lately). I have worked day in and day out, from sunrise to sunset. When something needs to be done, I see it's done. I have learned to plan, to be frugal in finances, to lead. Leadership is not something you are born with. You learn it and you earn it. Hey, that rhymes! Well, that's the way I see it. Don't you?

And what makes me really upset is this younger son of my father, he shows me no respect. I have to pull teeth to get him to do any work. His mind is always somewhere else. Did I mention he's always dreaming, never doing, like I am? I am the one who plans the day, purchases the materials and supplies we need just to operate the farm and the business, and the one who keeps the books. Nothing would ever get done if my father's youngest was in charge. I am sure you see what I am trying to say, don't you?

I'll tell you this, my father's other son is exceedingly difficult to get along with. He thinks he could do a better job than I can do. Would you believe his arrogance? He believes he is smarter than I am, that I am simply old-fashioned and out of touch with the "modern world." Can you imagine what this place would look like under his control—at least until he destroyed it? I don't know why my father puts up with him, but he does.

Speaking of my father, he is nice enough and really is a kind and friendly person. However, he is much too tolerant of his younger son. He does seem to genuinely appreciate all I do, but I wish he would realize that I have earned his respect and support. Look, I am not flashy. I'm really conservative on all matters—religion, finances, views, commitments—and I'm right. Some would say "real right!" So I am a little dull; dull is good, do you understand what I mean?

Well let me get back to that prodigal. Not too long ago he had the audacity to go to my father and ask for his inheritance. We're talking about a third of my father's estate—a third, mind you! What did he ever do to earn a third of anything? I was livid. I know our culture allows that, but I hate these new liberal ideas, don't you? I guess the idea is to make sure all the children get a share, simply by being born! I think the estate should be divided the fairest way: you get what you earn, like I will, of course!

So, away he went. He took his inheritance, walked out the door, marched down the road, shoulders held high, and set out to discover his fortune. What a joke! But he was sure in a hurry. It was obvious he wanted to get as far away from this place as fast as he could—and away from me, probably.

"Good riddance," is what I said. I would probably have preferred my father simply kick him out, throw him off of my—er, our—place without a shekel. Then we would see how he makes it in this world! Truthfully, the guy just got in the way around here. He was, and always will be, worthless.

From what I hear, he made lots and lots of new friends. Well, actually, he bought lots of new friends. My father's other son thought people liked him because he had a sense of freedom and adventure; he thought that he was a dreamer and a doer. I'm sure you don't believe that fantasy. These new friends liked him because he had quite a bit of money to spread around and he didn't mind throwing it away. Wouldn't you like him? Of course you would. I might have even liked him! Nah, I don't think so.

What a waste. No rules. Partying late into the night. No one like me was around to keep him in line. I'll bet he thought he was on top of the world. At least until the money ran out. For some reason, his new friends also disappeared after the money disappeared. What a shocker!

That prodigal! He wasted everything we had. All that money is gone now, as I understand it. But I'm not surprised; are you? Perhaps getting rid of him was worth it.

And if you think things couldn't get worse, wait until you hear what happened next. Guess what! There was a famine in the land. Money and work were scarce. He couldn't find a job! He wouldn't have known what to do if he had! He was destitute, people: a bum, a beggar. He was out of money, out of friends, and out of luck. And he deserved it all! The one person who really could have helped him, who could have put him back on the straight and narrow—me—was a long way off. I'll bet even I would have looked pretty good to him right then.

Then I heard he found a job feeding swine. What a tragedy! I nearly died laughing when I heard that. It doesn't get much lower than that. Can you image a Jew even being near those unclean animals? Well, that's what happens when you cavort with gentiles.

I was hoping my father's younger son would be so humiliated he would never entertain the thought of coming back here. I would have met him at the gate and sent him back to his fair-weather friends—and back to his pigs! That's what I would have done. He has never done a thing to deserve any compassion, any understanding.

But then there's my father. He is so gullible. I wish my father would see things my way. His younger son has our sheep's wool pulled over his eyes, that's obvious. I can imagine his other son coming down the road, hat in hand, head bowed down in mock humility, groveling about how sorry he is, and begging for forgiveness. It's enough to make one nauseous!

Well, you know what happened next: just what I predicted! I was not surprised to hear about that prodigal coming down the road. I was out in the field working. I'm always somewhere working. I had expected this day for a long time. And I had dreaded it for a long time, as well. I know my father all too well. He is so, so soft; so gullible. For me, you get one chance and that's it. No do-overs allowed.

And then guess what happened? It really upset me. There was my father, rushing down the road to meet that wayward, worthless, lazy reprobate.

In fact, my father ran so fast he could have had a heart attack. Of course, then I would have taken over completely. I could have thrown this other son of his out of this place forever. I shouldn't think these thoughts, should I? But I couldn't take it. I took off to work in another field, as far away as I could get from this debacle. Work, work, work! And what has it gotten me? Obviously, my father loves his other son a lot more than he loves me.

But the situation got even worse! I was told by one of my workers that my father immediately called out to his servants to quickly do three things. First, he told them to bring the best robe and put it on the scoundrel. Then, he told them to put a ring on his finger. Finally, he told them to put sandals on his feet. Now, lest you think these are insignificant matters, they are not.

The robe signifies royalty. The prodigal was seen as a prominent member of my father's household, even though he certainly did not deserve it.

The ring was not just an ordinary ring. It was a signet ring. A signet ring! It symbolizes authority, power. It is used to seal official documents, making them valid. One would press the family seal down on wax, so any reader would know the document was valid. The ring on his finger symbolized that he was recognized with authority as a true member of my father's family.

Finally, the sandals represented sonship. Sons wear sandals. Servants do not. By the robe, the ring, and the sandals, my father was saying that this person who had demeaned our family name was his son! As wayward as he had been, as foolishly as he had acted, my father still loved him and accepted him as his son! How could any father love someone who had betrayed his entire family? Do you understand what I am saying?

What did he ever do to be called a son? He certainly has not earned that right, as I have.

Not only that; for my father his return was a cause for celebration. He planned a party, invited his younger son's wayward friends and the neighbors, and prepared the fattened calf. It was an event fit for a king! It was certainly a deplorable waste.

My father, so gullible, so naïve, so...you fill in the blank. Besides, he never gave a party for me, never killed a fattened calf for me—not even a small goat!—and he never invited in my friends to celebrate with me. Besides, I don't have many friends.

My father reminds me of this teacher from Nazareth in Galilee I have been hearing about. This teacher says he has a way better than the Law? What could be better than the Law? Rules, regulations, everything is as clear as can be. I like that. I love the Law! Besides, and listen closely, if you know what you are doing, you can work your way around the Law. I know; I do it all the time. For example, one is allowed on the Sabbath to travel a short distance from home, a little over a half mile according to your standards. But I take a tent, travel the allowed distance, set up my tent and call it home. Then I travel the allowed distance again, and again set up my tent, my home. I keep doing this until I get where I want to go. And I have kept the law! Anyway, what a radical this teacher is! But I'll bet my father's youngest would like him. No responsibility, no accountability. I like that: "no account ability." That's pretty funny, even for a guy like me who has no sense of humor.

I was told that this teacher, I believe his name is Jesus, teaches his followers to pray to God like this: "Our Father who is in heaven." What a pathetic way of looking at God—as our father. I like a God who is a judge, an enforcer of his laws.

I hope this Jesus doesn't have my father in mind when he refers to God as "Father." Why would we need the Law? All one would have to do is go out and live a riotous life, then come crawling back, be forgiven, and be accepted into full sonship. I couldn't take that. You have to keep the Law. You have to earn God's love, don't you? I prefer the image of a great judge on his judgment seat, meting out punishment to the wayward reprobates of this world; that's what I like. Don't you?

But I have to admit, my father loves me. He went out to meet his sorry son when he came home. I would have stood on the porch, arms crossed, with a cold stare that would have drilled a hole right through him! But when I wouldn't go in and celebrate his other son's return, my father came out to talk with me. He met me on my turf, just like he did his other son.

He assured me that all was coming to me; all would be mine. That was really good news to me! He called his other son "my brother," something I just cannot bring myself to do. He told me that "my brother" was dead, but is now alive. If I could be sure my father loved me as much as he does his other son, then maybe I might accept what he is saying. But I am not sure.

He invited me in to join the celebration. What would you do? I think he was asking too much, don't you? Don't you?

Do you think all one has to do to be right with God is to confess his or her failures, shortcomings, and mistakes? All one needs to do is say he or she is unworthy and ask to simply be a servant in the Father's household. Is that all it takes? What do you think? Does God love us so much that he can forgive us no matter what we have done? I am having a real struggle with this idea. Does God's love overcome his demand for justice? I don't know. What do you think? What do you think? Here comes my father. I think he wants to say something to you. Maybe we can talk later? You know where to find me. I'll be out working.

FATHER: Well, there it is. You see how hard it is to be a father with two sons so different from each other. I love both of them. And it's not based upon who they are, or what they have done. My love is founded upon who I am. Parents, we love our children regardless of all the good or all the bad they do. And this will not change.

Maybe my understanding of what it means to be a father does have some spiritual truth to it. I think the prophet from Nazareth is right on target. God is our Father and we are his children. I am sure most of you listening to me understand exactly what I am saying. In fact, there is another parable about a lost coin. This woman has ten coins and loses one. She, with the help of her friends, looks and looks until the coin is found. The point of this story is that God searches for those who are lost, separated from him. Can God be not only fatherly, but as in this parable, also motherly at the same time? What do you think?

Think about my story and think about how God loves you as a son or a daughter, regardless of who you are and what you have done. Hopefully, all of you will recognize that your relationship with God will make you more humble, make you more aware of the Father's love, and make you realize how fortunate you are to be able to call God "our Father."

Welcome home, children!

NARRATOR: We have seen a delightful and instructive parable of Jesus through the eyes of its three characters. The teachings are always relevant. With God as our Father, we are all sisters and brothers in Christ. We are certainly different from each other, but we are a part of the same family: the family of God.

I remember seeing a small sign which read, "We don't have to be twins to be brothers!" How true that is! I think the parable of the prodigal son and the elder son bears witness to that truth. We are brothers and sisters and because of this we all need to learn from our one Father. We can love each other and also the world. We are truly one in the bond of love.

EXTRA OPTIONS:

Invocation: Our God, we come together on this day as your children. We depend upon your parental love. We approach you as unworthy, yet forgiven children. We rejoice in your forgiveness, rely upon your mercy, and are surrounded by your never-ending love.

We are gathered to worship you, to praise you through song, Scripture, prayer, and giving. We come to hear your Word, to proclaim your Word, and to commit to following your living Word in our daily lives.

We commit ourselves to seeing your world, to understanding that world, and to proclaiming in word and deed your genuine compassion for your world. Your son, Jesus, told us that you love the world so much, and that you have demonstrated that love by sending him, your Son, so that we might believe in him and have life everlasting.

So, on this day, let us worship you in hope and anticipation of all that lies before us individually and collectively. Lead us in being your children and in bringing honor and glory to you by the way that we live our lives. We ask this prayer in the name of Jesus, your Son and our brother. Amen.

Benediction: Recite the Lord's Prayer (Matthew 6:9-13):
Our Father who is in heaven, hallowed be your name.
Your kingdom come. Your will be done, on earth as it is in heaven.
Give us this day our daily bread.
And forgive us our debts, as we also have forgiven our debtors.
And do not lead us into temptation, but deliver us from evil. For yours is the kingdom and the power and the glory forever. Amen.
(paraphrase by Slayden Yarbrough)

MONOLOGUE 5: JOHN AND THE APOCALYPSE

TEXTS:

Revelation 1:1-3 – The revelation from Jesus Christ, which God gave him to show his servants what must soon take place. He made it known by sending his angel to his servant John, who testifies to everything he saw—that is, the word of God and the testimony of Jesus Christ. Blessed is the one who reads aloud the words of this prophecy, and blessed are those who hear it and take to heart what is written in it, because the time is near

Revelation 1:9-11 – I, John, your brother and fellow partaker in the tribulation and kingdom and perseverance which are in Jesus, was on the island called Patmos because of the word of God and the testimony of Jesus. I was in the Spirit on the Lord's day, and I heard behind me a loud voice like the sound of a trumpet, saying, "Write in a book what you see, and send it to the seven churches: to Ephesus and to Smyrna and to Pergamum and to Thyatira and to Sardis and to Philadelphia and to Laodicea.

Revelation 1:19 – Write, therefore, what you have seen, what is now and what will take place later.

INTRODUCTION:

In 2001 a popular radio evangelist predicted Jesus was going to return and set up his millennial kingdom on May 21. His organization purchased space on a huge billboard in a nearby city. The day came and went and there were no reports of any unusual happenings. The obvious conclusion was that he was wrong. The radio personality revised his date to October 31. Again, Jesus did not return. My prediction, based upon my understanding of the history of Christianity, was that Jesus would not return on either of these dates. Guess what, my predictions came true. Time and again prognosticators throughout history have predicted the exact date of the return of Jesus and not one of them has been correct.

You don't hear many sermons preached from the book of Revelation in the twenty-first century. And when you do, Revelation is usually interpreted as a book whose symbolism is used to prophetically predict what is going to happen in relation to the end of time. The vast majority of ministers who do preach on the book usually hold to a premillennial view, which asserts that after a period of great tribulation, Christ will return and set up a literal millennial, or one-thousand-year, kingdom on earth. Dispensational premillennialism, the most popular view, teaches that the church will be raptured up before the tribulation. In my early years as a Christian and a student I studied the Scofield Reference Bible, which worked out this entire system in great detail. I wanted to know the future and Revelation was interpreted as the key. Historical premillennialism teaches that the church will go through the tribulation. A number of my friends hold to this interpretation.

Another interpretation was popular at the turn from the nineteenth to the twentieth century when a very optimistic attitude was prevalent. Humanity had made major successes in science and technology. For example, the telephone and telegraph speeded up communication. Railroads and steamships changed the way we traveled. Church historian Kenneth Scott Latourette called the nineteenth century the Great Century.and it was in so many ways.

Religiously, there was a belief that man could make the world so much better and society's woes could be overcome. The Social Gospel arose with great hope, and many believed man could usher in the kingdom of Christ with a period of peace and perfection for a millennium, after which Christ would return.

In graduate school at Baylor University, I became interested in the history of Christianity, beginning with the life and ministry of Jesus and the rise of the early church. When interpreting the New Testament (as well as the Old Testament), I concluded it was important to understand the historical background of each writing, including the setting, the time, the audience, the purpose, and the response of the readers, if possible. I began to see Revelation in a whole new light. I saw the book as being written during the persecution of Emperor Domitian in the mid-nineties of the first century AD. Domitian was demanding all of his subjects worship him in the state temples as divine and to pray to him as Lord. I saw the seven churches of Asia mentioned by John as real churches with enormous challenges and weaknesses, as well as great potential. And I saw the millennium in a symbolic sense rather than a literal sense. I adopted the position of amillennialism, or as I prefer, "nonmillennialism."

This morning I want to present my interpretation through the eyes of John as he tells his story. So sit back and imagine a ninety-plus-year-old sage sharing with you his latest writing and telling you his story. Keep in mind, I am not addressing issues of authorship, but simply presenting this monologue by retelling the story in the first person as John.

MONOLOGUE: JOHN AND THE APOCALYPSE
Setting: Patmos, a small island off the coast of Asia in the Aegean Sea. It is the mid-nineties AD. John, a very old man, enters a room with several friends present. He looks tired, but conveys a deep sense of relief. In one hand he carries a scroll, which he holds up for his friends to see. He begins to speak.

JOHN: My good friends, here it is. It is finally finished: my latest, and probably my last writing. I am ready to add it to my Gospel and my many letters to my friends and our churches. Some of these, in fact, are being copied and are circulating among our people.

Perhaps the writing of the scroll is the reason I have outlived all the other apostles. Peter was executed in Rome by Nero. James, my brother, was martyred under Herod Agrippa I. And all the others, too, are now gone.

But it seems I have been spared for this moment in time, this monumental crisis which is threatening the continued existence of our churches. An old man like me, the last living eyewitness among the closest disciples of Jesus, kept alive so I could be around to encourage and challenge those persecuted saints upon whose shoulders the burden of the faith now rests.

These may be the most difficult days the church has ever faced. Do you think I am here on Patmos taking a vacation? No, I've been exiled to this place. Rome wants to keep me quiet. Rather than execute an old man, they sent me here to keep me out of trouble, hoping I would die. Can you imagine an old man past ninety being seen as a threat by the Roman Empire?

Now this emperor, Domitian, he's been around for about a decade and a half. He's quite different from other emperors. He claims to be divine! I know, and you know, the Roman Senate has declared deceased emperors to be divine. But Domitian claims to be a god while he is still living, and he expects all of his subjects to go to the state temples to burn incense and pray to him.

"Caesar is Lord." That's what he wants us to admit. Caesar is Lord! How absurd. How unacceptable! We Christians are good citizens. We pay our taxes. We try to live ethical and exemplary lives. We fulfill our responsibilities as good subjects of the Roman Empire. We even pray for Caesar. But we must never pray to him. He is not Lord! Jesus is Lord! We must never give to the state that which belongs to God alone!

But Domitian cannot understand how we can be good citizens and not worship him. He thinks we are treasonous. He fears for his empire, for his kingdom. And he is convinced it will all fall apart if every citizen does not call him Lord.

So he has commanded this physical assault upon the church, in a way we have never known. Some Jews have persecuted the followers of Jesus, and the populace has done the same from time to time. Every time there has been a fire, or a famine, or a plague, they blamed it on us. Some Romans believed their gods were angry at them for tolerating us. Some local officials accused us of violating local or Roman law, which we did not. Even Nero persecuted us when much of Rome burned. You know the story. He needed a scapegoat to take the heat off himself.

But now, especially here in Asia where we have worked so hard and for so long, now we see our very survival threatened. Why? The answer is simple. We won't worship the emperor.

We must not give in! We must not yield at any point on this issue. With courage and conviction, we must stand firm, even if it costs us our lives!

These are the reasons I have written this scroll, to encourage and rally the Christians of Asia to remain firm, to keep the faith regardless of the cost. Courage is the great Christian virtue, which is needed now.

This is no ordinary writing. I have chosen to present my message in apocalyptic language. What is apocalyptic language? Well, this literature has been around for centuries. Read Daniel and Zechariah for a few good examples from the ancient writings.

Apocalyptic writings use elaborate and mysterious symbolism. Many of my fellow Christians are quite familiar with symbols used in apocalyptic writings. They can understand my hidden message. I use names, numbers, animals, birds, precious gems, and metals. All have secret meanings for those who understand.

For example, when you read about Babylon, you are not reading about Babylon. You are reading about Rome. Do you remember Peter's first letter? At the end he encourages his readers to stand firm. And then he writes, "She who is at Babylon...sends you greetings." Peter was never in Babylon. But he was in Rome when Nero persecuted the Christians. And you know the tradition that says not only Peter, but also Paul, were executed by Nero. One has to be careful about accusing Rome of violence against Christians. But those who know the ancient history know Babylon persecuted the Jews. Rome, the new Babylon, is now assaulting the Christians.

Or take numbers; they all have a special meaning. Five or any multiple of it—ten or one thousand—means human completeness; six represents evil; seven symbolizes the union of earth and heaven; twelve is the number of spiritual or sacred completeness. When you read my scroll, remember what I have just said—when you read about the seven seals, or the seven trumpets, or the seven bowls of wrath, or the mark of the beast with the number 666, or the 144,000 (a multiple of twelve); or one thousand years. Don't forget that these numbers have symbolic meanings!

Why do I write like this? Why don't I just openly and clearly present my message? There are two reasons. First, my message calling for faithfulness, courage, and steadfastness during these difficult days must be proclaimed. Christians must know that God is sovereign and that he will vindicate his people if they are faithful. They must be assured Domitian and his successors will not always deceive the people on this matter of worshiping the emperor. Second, my message must be hidden. I cannot openly say Domitian is going to lose in this struggle. If Christians were caught with literature saying Rome (Babylon) would be overthrown, Domitian would be defeated, and Christianity would prevail, they would be in grave danger and surely risk losing their lives. But by using the symbolic language of apocalyptic literature I am able to both present my crucial message to Christians who understand my symbols, and at the same time protect my readers. After all, how many Roman officials do you know who can understand apocalyptic imagery? How many Christians in any age can make sense of what I say when I use apocalyptic symbolism?

In fact, that might be a good title for this scroll: "The Apocalypse," the revelation, the unveiling! I am unveiling God's message of the revelation of Jesus Christ, and what it means in light of the tragic circumstances now facing our churches.

My message is addressed to the seven churches of Asia. In a nutshell, Ephesus has left its first love. Smyrna is a church that is poor but rich in spirit. Pergamum dwells where the throne of Satan is located. Thyatira harbors a Jezebel. Sardis has a reputation for living but is dead. Philadelphia has an open door of opportunity. And Laodicea is neither hot nor cold, but lukewarm, tepid.

Look, these churches are not perfect, but name one throughout history which is, or will be. These churches all have their problems, their weaknesses, and their shortcomings. But they are in the heat of battle. The pressure to yield to Domitian is so great in Asia. In fact, the war—and it is spiritual warfare—may well be won or lost in Asia! These churches simply cannot give in! They must not!

And if they can stand in the face of this brutal opposition, then surely all churches and all Christians in all ages can stand, regardless of the circumstances. Most certainly their example will encourage others to keep the faith in difficult days, both now and in future days and generations to come. That includes your generation as well!

So, do you want to know what I say in this scroll? Well, I was instructed to write about the things which were (what I saw in my vision on Patmos) and about those things which are (messages for the seven churches of Asia). I addressed these messages to the churches' pastors, whom I call angels. I was candid and honest with them. Our hope lies in the endurance of these real churches, not in perfect congregations which don't exist. And I was told to write about the things which shall be, which is at the heart of my scroll.

Using all kinds of symbolism, I describe what is taking place right now in the churches in the Roman Empire. I describe being taken up to heaven. There in the court of heaven I portray the Lion of Judah and the Lamb of God—the Messiah and the Suffering Servant, if you will. He was the only one worthy to open the seven-sealed scroll. And then, using broken seals and sounding trumpets to convey the judgment of God, I was able to state clearly and with certainty that God and Christ are sovereign and that God rules. He is in control, and those who remain faithful to him will be vindicated by him. Those who become martyrs for the faith will be rewarded. They will be safe and in his presence forever and ever!

Remember, in passage after passage I use symbols to convey the tragedies and difficulties of this age. You must understand this truth in trying to interpret and apply my message to your generation. For example, the first four seals speak of the four horsemen of the apocalypse (white, red, black, and pale). They symbolize militaristic conquest, civil chaos, famine, and plague. The fifth seal represents the witnesses, the martyrs of the faith who die during the persecution, who want to know how long before God's justice will prevail. The sixth seal speaks of astronomical forces disturbing nature and the sealing of 144,000 from the tribes of Israel from these natural effects upon earth and the heavens. When taken literally the identification of the people who are part of this number will be misinterpreted in future centuries. Remember I am writing symbolically, not literally, to protect believers in my generation.

Beginning with chapter 12, I describe the second part of my vision, about how God will ultimately be victorious over Satan and the forces of evil. In the end the Messiah will appear, and God and the Messiah will rule over his kingdom forever and ever.

Again, please keep in mind that I am using symbolic language to hide my message from Roman authorities. I call Satan a dragon. I tell how he tries unsuccessfully to devour a woman's newborn child. The mother, of course, represents Israel, and the child is Christ. I place this battle in heaven. Understand that what is taking place on earth is a part of the greater cosmological struggle between good and evil! Then Satan is cast down to earth. And— listen carefully, for this is the heart of my message—Satan makes war upon the church, the followers of Jesus. This is what is happening now as I write!

How does he do this? He does it by means of two beasts. The first beast symbolizes the Roman emperor, Domitian, who demands all people worship him, including Christians. All of Domitian's subjects must acknowledge "Caesar is Lord." When they do not do so, persecution obviously follows.

The second beast is the official cult in charge of enforcing worship of the emperor through natural effects upon earth and the heavens. This beast uses economic boycott, deceit, and execution, if necessary, to carry out his duties. I use a secret code number for this beast: 666! You ask me, how did I come up with this number? Well, there is a rumor floating around that Emperor Nero will return to persecute the church. He was the first emperor to persecute Christians, you know, like Domitian is now doing. Now, if you understand Hebrew you know each letter has a numerical designation. Using this alphabet, consider "Nero Caesar": if you add up the designated number for each letter, the total comes out to be 666.

On the other hand, I am sure that I will really confuse so many interpreters throughout the history of Christianity with the number. I have no doubt that through the ages many will use mathematical gymnastics to interpret and identify 666 with some historical villain, perhaps a church leader or a politician. Remember once more, I am writing about the church in my day using symbolic language.

Back to my vision. Events will lead up to a future battle between the forces of God and Satan, the great battle of Armageddon. Of course, my prediction is that God will surely win. The first beast (imperial Rome) and the second beast (the official religious cult which enforces emperor worship) will be defeated and cast into the lake of fire. Satan, that old dragon, will be chained for one thousand years (read Revelation 20:1-6 carefully). Satan will no longer deceive the nations on the matter of emperor worship. Keep in mind, one thousand years is a symbol for a complete period of time. Satan will not deceive the nations to worship the emperor during this period. And those who became martyrs for the faith during the reign of Domitian will know peace.

But Satan will be freed again. He will try to challenge God with all he has. That will not be enough. In the end God will completely defeat him. Now, for those interested in the future, this is my prediction of the future. In the end God will defeat Satan once and for all and the church will know peace. The church through the ages will be with God forever in the New Jerusalem, with no pain, no sorrow, no tears, only joy and triumph. Don't you think this message will resonate with those who are facing the persecution of the Roman Empire and all of its power?

You may ask, how will this scroll be received? How will it be understood? I am sure some will find it confusing. They will throw their hands up in the air, say "I can't understand it," and avoid it like the plague. Again predicting the future, do you know the name John Calvin, the Protestant reformer from Geneva? Look at his commentaries on the books of the Bible. There is not one on Revelation. Why? He found it to be too confusing. So, he avoided a commentary on the Apocalypse.

I also suppose there will be others who read more into the scroll than there really is. I know some will surely try and mix symbolism with literalism. Some things they will interpret symbolically, others literally. There are some who are will look for a literal earthly kingdom of one thousand years, the millennial reign of Christ and his church on earth.

But I remind you, Jesus said his kingdom is not of this world; it is spiritual, and its power is in serving, not in the sword, not in governmental authority. My brother James and I initially saw his kingdom as earthly, and we were criticized by Jesus because of this. In our arrogance we wanted to sit on the right hand and the left hand of Jesus, sharing in his earthly power. In our youthful exuberance we wanted to bring down fire from heaven on opponents of Jesus. In fact, some called us "Sons of Thunder." But after the death and resurrection of Jesus, we understood clearly what he was really saying. His kingdom was to be found in the hearts of the believers, not in earthly authority! So, read my lips: "He who lives by the sword, dies by the sword!"

Some will interpret this scroll as a plan for all of the ages, spelling out in detail all that will take place. But it is not a plan for the ages. It is a blueprint for survival. The real future of the church is in our hands right now at the time of this writing, when the real hope for survival of the church rests in our hands. Why would I look down the tunnel of time? How we respond to the challenge from Domitian, who is threatening our existence, is the crisis I am addressing. If the church of Jesus doesn't survive in my time, there may be no church in later centuries, like your twenty-first century!

My friends, your faithfulness is necessary now. The church is in grave danger. The faith is being threatened as never before. You cannot stargaze and be faithful.

Now, with all of the courage you can muster, with all of the conviction you have, you must give witness and testimony to Christ. There are untold pressures on the church, risk around every corner, and challenges at each moment. Dare you concentrate so much on the future when the battle for your survival is now?

To my people, keep the faith. Give witness to Christ with the totality of your lives. Stand firm as never before. My message is quite clear for my generation, and for all generations that will follow. As I told you previously, courage is the Christian virtue to be practiced; cowardice is the great sin to be avoided, the great vice in times of struggle.

You cannot lose the fight now or there will be no future. As God's people you must stand firm and hold onto the faith tighter and more convincingly than ever before. You must be willing to pay the price for yourselves, for Christ, and for those who will follow you in the years ahead.

This is the message of my scroll for my troublesome days, and for those days of trial like yours, which will surely come. You must be God's people today, and He will be your help forever and ever. Amen!

EXTRA OPTIONS

Invocation: Our God, we invoke your presence on this Lord's Day as we gather together to worship you. We acknowledge that you are the God of our past, our history. Lead us to learn from your witnesses who came before us. As we learn from the prophets of old, through the teachings and example of Jesus, and throughout the testimony from the ages of the church, instill in us a commitment to learn more about you.

We affirm that you are the God of our present. Continue to make us aware that you are at work in this time and in this place. Stir a passion in us, a desire to be a relevant people, understanding the world around us and shaping our ministry and message to bear witness to all we encounter. Strengthen us to live lives that affirm and honor you in this time where you have placed us. And as we learn from our past, let us never forget that Jesus, your Son, is our Lord here and now.

Point our hearts and minds to the future. You have called us individually and collectively to affirm your grace, forgiveness, mercy, and love to those around us now, and in the days and years ahead. Make us aware that we are stewards of the good news we have received and continue to cherish for our children and grandchildren.

So, on this day, let us worship you with our hearts and souls and minds and strengths. In the name of Jesus, the Lord for all times. Amen!

Benediction: Join with me in sharing with one another the ancient benediction we call the peace of Christ. Turn to your neighbor and say, "May the peace of Christ be with you!" Let us go forth in that peace. Amen.

MONOLOGUE 6: A VISIT WITH MARTIN LUTHER

TEXTS:

Habakkuk 2:4 (NASB[4]) – Behold, as for the proud one, his soul is not right within him; But the righteous will live by his faith.

Galatians 2:16 – Nevertheless knowing that a man is not justified by the works of the Law but through faith in Christ Jesus, even we have believed in Christ Jesus, so that we may be justified by faith in Christ and not by the works of the Law; since by the works of the Law no flesh will be justified.

MONOLOGUE: A VISIT WITH MARTIN LUTHER

Guten Morgen! Wie gehen sie? Ich bin Martin Luther. Sprechen Duetsche? Nein? Nichts sehr gut? Ein bitte? Maybe I ought to speak in English; this is the language you speak, is it not? Good morning! Let me introduce myself. I am Martin Luther from Saxony. I am delighted to have this opportunity to visit with you today.

Actually, I am here to help you celebrate Reformation Sunday, a day for which I am the source of inspiration. In fact, Halloween this year—the eve of All Saints Day—is more than five hundred years since the beginning of the Reformation. Quite an accomplishment I would say! So, I've been invited here to share my story. It's been pushing 500 years since I spoke to a congregation, since I died in 1554. I had several vocations: student, potential lawyer, monk, teacher, reformer, and as Pope Leo X called me, "a wild boar in his master's vineyard."

I was born November 10, 1483. Soon you can celebrate my birthday. I was born and died in Eisleben in Saxony. I had gone back to assist in resolving a dispute in the town, became ill, and passed away just a short distance from where my mother had delivered me.

Ah, my mother, Margaretta—she was of peasant stock, as was my father, Hans. She was quite superstitious. She believed in goblins and other little creatures who stole vegetables, fruit, and eggs. I never got away from my beliefs in ghosts and demons, but I reflected the beliefs common in my day—as you do yours as well, I'm quite sure.

Hans, my father, became a small, petty capitalist in the mining industry near Mansfield. He was able to provide me with a good education. I graduated with a bachelor's degree from the University of Erfurt in 1502 and received a master's degree in 1505. Later, in 1512, I earned a doctorate in theology from the University of Wittenberg.

Upon obtaining my master's degree, I received from my father a gift of one of the most important law books of the time. He had great hopes that I would succeed. Furthermore, he and my mother depended upon me to care for them during their later years. But to his great disappointment, and I mean great disappointment, this was not to be.

To understand what happened and why, one has to understand the religious climate of the sixteenth century. Religion so often focused upon fear. God and Christ were portrayed as ready to pronounce judgment at any moment upon an unrepentant sinner. Paintings of Christ often portrayed him with a sword in his hand or clinched between his teeth.

There was not much hope for relief from the anxiety caused by this view. One had to be in good stead with the church; a well-known Latin saying was *nulla salus, extra ecclesiam,* translated "no salvation outside the church." The church administered the sacraments and the sacraments conveyed the grace of God. Get yourself excommunicated from the church, and prepare for an eternity in hell. And even if you made it to heaven, you had to get there by way of purgatory, an in-between place where one was punished for unforgiven sins against the church.

In my day we believed the sin and guilt of Adam was present in everyone at birth. Baptism washed away original sin and all sins up to one's baptism. But what about sins committed after one was baptized? The sacrament of penance took care of that. You also needed to realize that when you sinned, it was not only against God but also against the church. God could forgive you and the priest would pronounce God's forgiveness. But you had to make some kind of retribution for your sin against the church.

This is where penance came into play. There were four stages to this sacrament. First, you were contrite. You were expected to be sorrowful for what you had done. Then you confessed your sin, not only to God, but also to your priest. Initially, you would then perform some act of satisfaction to pay the price for your sin, to balance the scales. You might go on a pilgrimage, do some good deed, offer special prayers, make a special contribution to your church, or perform some other visible expression of your genuine contrition. Then the priest would pronounce absolution from the punishment of your sin. As time passed, the church reversed stages three and four. The priest would pronounce absolution to be validated once you performed your act of satisfaction.

But what if one could not perform an act of satisfaction at the appropriate time? This concern led to another issue of disagreement during my lifetime, which was over what the church called the "Treasury of Merit" or the "Treasury of the Saints." The church taught that Jesus, the apostles and the saints, and the university religion professors (a university professor of religion joke; I as the author of this monologue was a university professor) lived really good lives, so there was extra merit left over. Poor saints like you could use this merit to reduce or eliminate time spent in purgatory if you could not meet a required act of satisfaction. The way to access (that's a good twenty-first century term) the Treasury of Merit was to purchase an indulgence. This was a paper document stating that you had paid for the indulgence, and you were due to receive all of the benefits attained therein! Keep this in mind as I continue.

But let me get back to my story. I was headed toward a career in law. But two things happened that changed my plans. First, a close friend about my age died suddenly. This resulted in great fear for my own life. Did God punish my friend with death for his sins? If so, might he not do the same to me? The second event occurred in July of 1505. I was walking near Stotternheim when a thunderstorm developed. Lighting struck near me and I was knocked to the ground. I truly thought God was trying to kill me! I cried out for help, not to God but to St. Anne, the patroness saint of the miners and the mother of Mary. You dared not approach God directly. Anyway, I made a vow, crying out, "St. Anne, help me, I will become a monk." I was absolutely scared to death and absolutely serious. Perhaps with the intervention of St. Anne and the pledge to enter a monastery, God might spare my life.

I survived the lightning bolt, shaken but true to my vow. A short time later I entered the Augustinian monastery at Erfurt, much to the dismay of my father. I chose this monastery because of the strict discipline of the order. Many monasteries had gotten soft, but my dilemma was too serious for me to choose an easy path of life.

I was a good monk. In fact, I later surmised that if anyone could be saved by "monkery" I certainly would have been. I did everything required of me. I prayed. I studied. I worked diligently. I performed the mass when assigned, although it frightened me greatly and I barely got through it the first time. I even walked to Rome in 1510-1511 to represent my monastery in a dispute within the Augustinian order. I was greatly disappointed at the flippant attitude toward religion and the sacraments of the church of so many there.

Perhaps it was here when I began to question for the first time the teachings of the church. The church claimed it had brought the stairs of Pilate's judgment hall from Jerusalem to Rome, the same stairs Jesus ascended to appear before the Roman procurator. It was taught that if you climbed the stairs on your knees and said a *pater nostra*—or as you call it, the "Lord's Prayer"—on each step, when you reached the top a soul would be released from purgatory. When I reached the top, I asked myself concerning this belief, "Who knows whether it is so?" Doubt is often the beginning of deliverance!

Back at the monastery I practiced self-denial like no other monk. On cold nights I would sleep without sufficient covering in an act of asceticism that endangered my health. I confessed every sin to my superior, Johann von Staupitz. I got to the point of even confessing unknown sins, just in case I left some out. I feared God like no other could fear him. I didn't want to take any chances.

I became a real nuisance. In your day you might me call me a basket case. I had gone off the deep end spiritually, emotionally, psychologically. What do you do with one who has reached the edge of his limits? What do you do with someone who is suffering from spiritual, emotional, and psychological insecurities of the highest order? Johann von Staupitz, my superior, knew what to do. He assigned me to teach religion at a university!

Actually, looking back I realize he knew exactly what he was doing. I began to teach courses in the Bible. And, of course, studying the biblical books was an important part of carrying out my responsibilities. In 1513 I taught the Psalms. In Psalm 22, I realized for the first time that Jesus died for all of us, for you, for me. He carried our burden. The psalm reads, "My God, my God, why have you forsaken me?" Jesus cited this verse during his crucifixion. For the first time, I began to realize I could not earn my salvation, but that Jesus had already provided the way to God for me.

In 1515 I taught Paul's letter to the Romans and in 1516 I taught Paul's letter to the churches of Galatia. In these two books, I discovered the marvelous teaching that resolved so many of my concerns. This teaching was that "the just shall live by faith alone." How are we made right with God? Not through the sacraments administered by the priesthood of the church. Not through the disciplined life of the monk. Rather we are made right with God through a confident, trusting, simple faith in the redemptive work of Jesus. That's it. It is just that simple. Salvation is a gift. I discovered this, I believed this, and I found the peace for which I had so long sought.

The university life also provided the environment in which I began to call for reforms of the church. As early as 1516, I questioned the doctrine of indulgences, as others had done, and preached against them on three occasions, including the eve of All Saints Day that year. In fact, my ruler Frederick the Elector, a dedicated religious man, had collected many relics whose merits were available through the sale of indulgences. Each relic had been assigned a value for released time in purgatory, for a total that reached 1,902,202 years! As a matter of fact, my salary was paid by the sale of indulgences, the very practice against which I was openly preaching! I think I was rather courageous, don't you?

Well, in 1517 Pope Leo X sold the position of Archbishop of Mainz to Albert of Brandenburg. The story goes that Leo wanted 12,000 ducats to honor the twelve apostles, and Albert offered 7,000 in praise of the seven deadly sins. They agreed upon 10,000 ducats, presumably not for the Ten Commandments! In order to enable Albert to pay for the position and to obtain money for the building of St. Peter's Cathedral in Rome, the pope declared a special sale of indulgences in Albert's domain. Half of the profits would go to the pope for St. Peter's and half would go to Albert, who would then forward his share on to the pope to pay for his new position.

A Dominican monk named John Tetzel was assigned the task of hawking the sale of these indulgences. He was good, extremely good. Actually, he was too good! He didn't come into Saxony, where I lived and taught, but set up just across the border. Many persons from Saxony would cross over to purchase what Tetzel had to offer. He would go into a town and set up his stand with a coffer in front of him. A coffer was a large, rectangular box with a dish on top and a slit where the coins could be deposited. After an impassioned plea to the hearers to purchase an indulgence that would release loved ones from purgatory, Tetzel would conclude with a jingle: "When the coin in the coffer rings, the soul from purgatory springs!" In fact, some accused Tetzel of changing the stages of penance to "contrition, confession, and contribution"!

Tetzel made other extravagant claims, many of which were rejected by the church, and others that were open to debate. One of my favorite stories tells of the time a man asked Tetzel if he could purchase an indulgence to take care of the punishment for a sin that he planned to commit. Tetzel quickly responded, "Yes, if you buy it now!" Did I tell you he was a really good salesman of indulgences? The man purchased the indulgence. Later, he followed Tetzel out of town, robbed him, beat him up, and then proclaimed, "This is the sin which I had planned to commit!" I doubt the story is true—but I hope it is!

Tetzel's activities and claims caused me to challenge the idea of indulgences. On October 31, 1517, the eve of All Saints Day, or Halloween, I posted on the door of the Castle Church at Wittenberg what is known as my 95 Theses. In this document I stated that the belief in indulgences was inconsistent with the teachings of the New Testament and I denied the concept of the Treasury of Merit. All I really wanted to do was to have a debate over the issues. Posting theses calling for debates on controversial issues was a common practice during my day.

Well, some of my friends translated the 95 Theses from Latin into German, had them printed, and distributed them throughout Saxony. I hope you realize how important the invention of the printing press in the previous century was to the Reformation. It was as impactful then as the internet has been during your time. Anyway, a simple initiative for a debate soon exploded into a major controversy and it seemed like everyone was after me.

During 1520 I published three works that were at the heart of the Reformation, which historians have concluded began on October 31, 1517 with the posting of the 95 Theses. I wrote the *Address to the German Nobility*, defending the authority of the civil officials over the papacy and calling upon them to implement the reforms I was proposing. My *Babylonian Captivity of the Church* dealt with the sacramental system of the church, and I reduced the number of sacraments from seven to two. In *On the Freedom of the Christian*, I magnified the freedom of every believer and defended the priesthood of each believer and the doctrine of justification by faith alone, the central doctrine of the Reformation.

I was soon called to appear before Charles V, the Holy Roman Emperor, at the Diet of Worms in 1521. I was asked to recant my positions. I considered this request carefully. My response was, "Here I stand. I can do no other. God help me!" When you truly believe what you teach, there may come a time when your commitment to those beliefs is tested. This was one of those times for me. Roland Bainton, a twentieth century historian, titled his biography of me, *Here I Stand*. My defense resulted in grave dangers for me. I was excommunicated from the church and banned as an outlaw by the state, which meant anyone could put me to death.

Fortunately, while the politicians were debating other matters, my friends smuggled me out of town and took me to Wartburg Castle. I grew a beard and went into hiding under the name of Knight George. I spent eleven months at Wartburg and began to translate the Bible into German. One of the great contributions of the Reformation is the translation and printing of the New Testament into the vernacular of the people. Of course, the Bible was the source of written authority for the Reformation. The concept of *sola scriptura* rejected the Roman Catholic claim of authority based upon the Scriptures and the tradition of the church. When you call for reform, when you begin a revolt, you need a source for justification. Mine was the Bible.

Meanwhile, things were getting out of hand in Wittenberg, so in 1522 I returned there at the risk of my own life. A group called the Zwickau Prophets had stirred up riots by the breaking of images and the destruction of paintings. They were a chiliastic group, anticipating the return of Christ and justifying all kinds of militant and destructive actions based upon their beliefs. I can't tell you how many times groups like these have caused chaos in the years since the Reformation. The things people justify when they are convinced they know what is going to happen, and when it will happen. I can tell you this: I didn't know then and I don't know now when all of these things might happen, or if they will. Well, I calmed the city down, stating, "Faith produces works of love and order, not works of hatred and disorder."

Advances and setbacks for the Reformation took place in the years that followed. In the end, however, the Reformation succeeded. Saxony became a Protestant state. An agreement was reached based upon the position that the religion of the prince would be the religion of the people. By the time of my death, the Reformation was well established and there would be no return to the old ways.

Other reform movements would appear beyond Germany among the Swiss, led initially by Huldrech Zwingli and then John Calvin. At one point when things were going badly for the Reformation, Zwingli and I met at Marburg to consider uniting. We agreed on fourteen-and-a-half points but disagreed on the interpretation of the Lord's Supper. He had a strange view, saying it was a symbolic memorial. Can you imagine holding this position? Of course you can. Many religious groups accept the same view.

A left-wing group called the Anabaptists would soon appear in several regions, including the Swiss provinces, Germany, Austria, and the Netherlands. They rejected any union of church and state. They were a peculiar bunch, holding to baptism of believers only, congregational church government, and religious liberty.

In England reform took place when Henry VIII wanted to get a divorce from Catherine of Aragon. Henry had earlier been awarded the title "Defender of the Faith" by the pope for his efforts in opposing my reforms! He got his divorce by splitting from the Roman Church. It took a while, but real reforms took place under Edward VI and his half sister, Elizabeth I.

There are a few points I need to make. In 1525 I married a runaway nun named Catherine von Bora. I helped in her escape and tried to find her a husband. She insisted I be the one. I was fearing for my life and resisted for her sake. But thankfully she persisted, and she became an enormous help to me. My dear Katy ran our household, produced six children, and managed a farm. She brought joy to my life and contributed greatly to my success. I was able to complete the translation of the entire Bible in 1534, which was then used to teach the German language.

I must also confess, on this All Saints Day, that I was no saint. I had a number of flaws. I suffered from depression on many occasions. I sometimes became emotional. I am sure many of you know the story of my throwing the inkwell at the devil!

As I look back, I realize I was significantly intolerant. Do you know that this is often true of those of us in religious life? We become so convinced of the certainty of our beliefs and practices that we narrow the boundaries for those we consider to be truly on God's side; of course, we always are. And I was unquestionably anti-Semitic. I could try and justify it by arguing, as other Christians did during my day, that the Jews were the ones who sacrificed Jesus and therefore deserved no mercy or sympathy.

But as I look back, I realize I was wrong. Yet I find satisfaction in the fact that my journey eventually contributed to greater tolerance of other religious groups in later generations.

I tried to empathize with the peasants who were being mistreated by nobility during my time. In fact, they saw me as a potential champion of their cause in the early days of their movement. Initially, I wrote a work entitled *Admonition to Peace*, urging the authorities to grant the just claims of the peasants. But when they revolted in 1525, I could not remain sympathetic with their cause. I believed in an orderly society. Involvement in a militant rebellion would have destroyed my reforming movement of the church. I wrote another work addressing these new realities. My title suggests a subtle change of heart and a basic intolerance with the Peasant's Revolt: it was called *Against the Robbing and Murdering Peasant Gangs*! My advice was, "Let him who can, smite, slay, and stab" the "mad dogs." Was I a little too intolerant? Of course I was. I basically said to the princes, "Now control them any way you can." On May 15, 1525, 50,000 peasants were stopped cold at Frankenhausen. I am certain now that if I lived during your age I could not justify these actions, even in the name of God and the reformation of his church.

Let me conclude with a few final thoughts. I need to get back to the positive. As you remember the Reformation in the twenty-first century, over five hundred years after I posted my 95 Theses, whether you realize it or not you continue to believe and practice some of the basic teachings that I and other reformers of the sixteenth century struggled to implement and uphold.

For instance, you have consistently believed in justification by faith alone, and I commend you for this. This doctrine was the foundation of the Reformation. In fact, there have been so many reforms since my time that have focused on this significant biblical teaching, it has certainly opened my eyes. It was a significant part of the teachings of John Calvin and the Anabaptists, although we did not treat the latter kindly. The Great Awakening in New England began in 1734 in Northampton, Massachusetts, when Jonathan Edwards preached a series of sermons on "justification by faith." John Wesley, wanting to be a good servant of God, came from England to Georgia as a missionary, but only after he heard a Moravian preacher speak on the subject of justification by faith, based upon the preface of my commentary on Romans, did he begin to truly understand God's grace and move forward as one of the outstanding leaders of his day. Look at the place of this doctrine in Reinhold Niebuhr's teachings as he grappled with making the gospel relevant in the mid-twentieth century in the urbanized and industry-dominated Detroit. From Habakkuk to Paul to Augustine, and through the Reformation up to the present day, the relevancy of this doctrine is front and center. My advice is that when you start to get out of focus, return to the simplicity of this wonderful biblical and Reformation teaching.

The priesthood of all believers is one of my favorite doctrines. It has occupied a central place in Protestant teachings. You need no authority to stand before God save that of the lordship of Christ. I discovered that the grace of God is not administered by the priesthood through the sacraments of the church, but by approaching God through trusting faith. Yet, we can all serve as priests to others as we demonstrate and share God's love and grace to them. Sadly, there are those who have forgotten this teaching. In recent years there are voices of pastors who preach, "Trust me, trust me. I am the one who really knows what is good for you. I am the one who will keep you on the straight and narrow, and I do mean the straight and narrow." Don't forfeit your belief in the priesthood of the believer for the priesthood of the pastor. Should this happen to you, remember your roots and return to this precious biblical teaching. It will benefit and enrich, not only you, but also your pastors.

Believers through the centuries have done a good job of remaining committed to *sola scriptura*, the sole authority of the Bible in matters of faith and practice. Yet, you fight over the Bible too much. In your exuberance and commitment to the written Word you often miss the point that the Scriptures testify of God and his redemptive work, especially in the living Word, Jesus Christ. In so doing, in the name of biblical authority, you too often justify unbiblical attitudes and practices. But the Bible will continue to be a major starting point to understanding God and his love for you.

And don't forget the price I and others paid so each one of you would have the right and the duty to study and interpret the Scriptures for yourself. Don't forget how I committed my time and effort in translating the Bible into the language of my people and my reason for doing so. And don't forget, just because you read and study a Bible in your own language, your interpretations will not be inerrant and infallible. Listen to diverse views and learn. Work at applying the teaching of the Bible rather than trying to force others into conformity according to your own interpretations.

I need to conclude before I put you to sleep or before I get myself into trouble—again! Thank you for allowing me to visit with you on Reformation Sunday. Please forgive me of my failures. Do not be afraid to risk. You owe this in remembering my generation and in leading yours. You are indebted to future generations to build upon the foundations of the past and to pass on a faith much better than the one I have passed on to you.

Guten tag! Good day! I hopefully will see you in another time and another place.

EXTRA OPTIONS

Invocation: Our God, on this Sunday we are gathered together and are reminded of your abundant grace which becomes ours through simple faith in Jesus. We are so thankful that you accept us through faith alone. We are humbled knowing we cannot earn our salvation, and yet you have provided the way through the life of Jesus, your incarnate Word. Your message is so clear and so simple. You have set us free through faith in order to be free, as Paul says in Galatians 5:1. We are grateful that you trust us to exercise our faith in presenting the love and grace of Jesus in new ways to respond to our contemporary world. Although we are unworthy, you have set us free to be witnesses to Jesus in Jerusalem, Judaea, Samaria, in this place we call home, and to the ends of the earth,

On this Lord's Day we experience your presence in our midst. We know you accept our worship of you however we express it; in song, in prayer, and in giving. Unite us as we reflect upon you and your word, both written and incarnate, and upon our ministry in this place.

So once more, thank you God for justifying us through faith alone. We thank you for your love and grace, which enables us to be your children. We thank you for the gift of Jesus, who through his life and ministry and through his gift of the Spirit empowers us to serve and minister in this time and in this community. Amen.

Benediction: But the fruit of the Spirit is love, joy, peace, patience, kindness, goodness, faithfulness, gentleness, and self-control. Against such things there is no law. (Gal. 5:22-23 NASB)

DRAMATIC READING 1: I AM CHRISTMAS

NARRATOR OR PASTOR: Let us once more hear the Christmas story found in Luke's Good News.

Now in those days a decree went out from Caesar Augustus, that a census be taken of all the inhabited earth. This was the first census taken while Quirinius was governor of Syria. And everyone was on his way to register for the census, each to his own city. Joseph also went up from Galilee, from the city of Nazareth, to Judea, to the city of David which is called Bethlehem, because he was of the house and family of David, in order to register along with Mary, who was engaged to him, and was with child. While they were there, the days were completed for her to give birth. And she gave birth to her firstborn son; and she wrapped Him in cloths, and laid Him in a manger, because there was no room for them in the inn.

In the same region there were some shepherds staying out in the fields and keeping watch over their flock by night. And an angel of the Lord suddenly stood before them, and the glory of the Lord shone around them; and they were terribly frightened. But the angel said to them, "Do not be afraid; for behold, I bring you good news of great joy which will be for all the people; for today in the city of David there has been born for you a Savior, who is Christ the Lord. This will be a sign for you: you will find a baby wrapped in cloths and lying in a manger." And suddenly there appeared with the angel a multitude of the heavenly host praising God and saying,

"Glory to God in the highest, and on earth peace among men with whom He is pleased." (Luke 2:1-14 NASB)

I am Christmas. I am history and I am tradition, all woven together. Over two millennia have passed since my star illumined the sky over Bethlehem, directing to the Christ child all who would come and see. My significance is celebrated in numerous ways. Some read my story in the simplicity of a home warmed by an evening fire. Some prepare for my celebration by reading an advent book, or by the lighting of advent candles. Many unite with others to remember and praise the Christ child.

From the unadorned worship in a small, wood-framed structure of a country church, where age-old carols are loudly and joyously sung and my ancient story is repeated with renewed freshness in a simple parson's sermon, to a magnificent cathedral whose pipe organ reverberates amidst the beauty of stained glass windows and marble columns that rise to the heavens, whose music provides direction for other instruments, a choir, and talented soloists who perform a majestic cantata which reminds all who hear it of God's incarnate Word—in these diverse forms, my story is passed on from generation to generation.

Some look forward to strings of brightly colored lights surrounding old and new ornaments decorating a carefully selected tree. Some anticipate spiced cider and eggnog, pastries, nuts, and fruit, or red-and-white striped candy canes. Some love the carols, lighted candles, or nativity scenes. Others find warmth in the fellowship of old friends or relatives who have traveled long distances. Sadly, for some, Christmas is only crowded stores, long lines, and overdue bills, a reminder of unpleasant memories and missing love.

For all, however, my purpose is to remind men, women, and children that God loves you and that he has revealed his love by becoming one of you. This and this alone demonstrates the true significance of all you do to celebrate my season. I am Christmas and I come to you once more with a message of hope, of love, and of peace.

I am Christmas. I am the day celebrated to commemorate the birth of the Christ child. I am celebrated every year on December 25 throughout the world. I am over two thousand years old, yet my relevance is as contemporary as the breaking news.

I am Christmas. My day was spoken of by the prophets of old. Isaiah signaled my arrival when he wrote:

> For to us a child is born, to us a son is given, and the government will be on his shoulders. And he will be called Wonderful Counselor, Mighty God, Everlasting Father, Prince of Peace.Of the increase of his government and peace, there will be no end. He will reign on David's throne and over his kingdom, Establishing it with justice and righteousness from that time on and forever. (Isaiah 9:6-7, NIV)

Isaiah also predicted that:

> A shoot shall come from the stump of Jesse;
> From his roots a Branch will bear fruit.
> The Spirit of the Lord will rest on him –

> The Spirit of wisdom and understand-
> ing, the Spirit of counsel and power,
> The Spirit of knowledge and the fear of the Lord –
> And he will delight in the fear of the Lord. (Isaiah
> 11:1-3, NIV)

And now let us hear the story of the birth of the Christ child from those who were participants in this magnificent event.

AUGUSTUS CAESAR: Friends, Romans, and Countrymen, lend me your ears! I am Christmas. I am Augustus Caesar! I am the ruler of the great Roman Empire! And don't you forget it! I am the most powerful ruler in the Mediterranean world! I govern the Roman Empire! Nations and kings look to me in respect—and in fear. My power and my authority cannot be challenged by any other! How dare they to even think of it! My world is a Roman world in government. My world is a peaceful world, for none dare challenge the power of the Roman military. My world is a Hellenistic (or Greek) world in culture, including language, which enables communication throughout my empire among all of the diverse people who answer to me. It is to my capital that those who seek favor and prosperity travel. The phrase "all roads lead to Rome" is no idle claim. Travelers from Egypt and Asia, from North Africa and the barbarian territories look to me and the splendor of this city with respect. And did I say fear?

A small, insignificant part of my world is a Jewish world called Palestine. Those who rule there, like Herod, and Quirinius who governs Syria, have been appointed by me. They answer to me! I demand that they keep the peace, they collect taxes to support their work and my government, and they subject all of their people to my rule! None is so powerful, so important as I am? Do you not agree?

So, what does the birth of a Jewish boy mean to me? Nothing! Can this child challenge my rule? Of course he can't. Can this child insist upon the allegiance of millions, like I can? Don't make me laugh! The world will long remember me when I am gone. Can you possibly say that, can you possibly believe that, about this insignificant Jewish child, born in a stable, surrounded not by royalty but by shepherds and animals of the field? Of course not!

I am Augustus Caesar, the ruler of the Roman Empire, and no Jewish child can ever challenge me, or those who succeed me. Or can he?

ELIZABETH: I am Christmas. I am Elizabeth. I am the mother of a newborn named John, whose birth came as a complete surprise. My husband Zacharias and I are old, too old to become parents. And yet, this is exactly what took place. Zacharias, a priest, was chosen by casting lots to enter the temple and burn incense. It was there in the temple that an angel of the Lord appeared and told him we would have a son, John, who would be filled with the Spirit, who would be a forerunner of the long awaited Messiah, and who would call the people back to God.

Zacharias questioned this announcement, and why not? It seemed so absurd! So unbelievable! And what did his doubting get him? He was unable to speak until the birth of our son. That's quite a restriction, for a man of God to be silent for so long! I'm sure you agree?

But there is more to the story. Mary, my much younger cousin, also found favor with God in the most unusual circumstances and was promised a son as well. Her situation...well, I'll let her speak for herself shortly. She can tell her story much better than I.

As for me, John was born, and I shall always be amazed as to why God showed favor to me and Zacharias.

BETHLEHEM: I am Christmas. I am Bethlehem. I am a small town in Judea, a few miles from Jerusalem. I was the home of

Ruth and Boaz; and the home of David, the greatest king of Israel; and the burial place of Rachel, Jacob's wife and the mother of Joseph and Benjamin. It was the prophet Micah who predicted long ago that a ruler over Israel would come from me, small though I might be. And it is on this day, here in my town, that a child named Jesus will be born to a young woman named Mary, who is pledged to Joseph.

Have you ever considered how thought-provoking it is that God chose to become a man when he wanted to reveal himself most fully, most completely? God did not send mankind a book telling them who he was. He did not send you a set of principles or rules by which you should govern your lives. No. He became one of you. He entered into the mainstream of humanity and history, just as you did. He came in the birth of an infant, a child named Jesus who was born to Mary. This child grew and matured just as you should do, in all phases of life. The Gospel writer Luke tells you Jesus grew in wisdom and in stature, and in favor with God and man (Luke 2:52). What Luke is telling you is that Jesus grew up intellectually, physically, spiritually, and socially.

And why did he become a man? Why did this Word of God become incarnate? Because as a man, he could communicate more effectively than by any other means the message he wanted you to know and understand in order that you could receive his love and redemption. Well, enough of my sermonizing. There are others who want to tell you their stories.

THE INNKEEPER: I am Christmas. I am the innkeeper in Bethlehem. My inn is full tonight. There are many travelers in the land thanks to the census being taken by Augustus Caesar for taxation purposes, so you must arrive early if you expect to find a place to sleep here. Tonight, unfortunately, there are no rooms left. But the hour is late, and I suppose the stable in the shelter of a cave is better than no shelter at all.

One would expect a king to be born in a palace. But this young prince is not like most royalty, and his kingdom is not like those of this world. One would expect a prince to be clothed in the finest cloth and laid in the most expensive bed available. But this future king was wrapped in inexpensive material—swaddling cloth it is called—and placed on new straw in a manger. He was surrounded not by servants and handmaidens, but by farm animals in the coolness of the night air. Yet even this inconspicuous beginning would not go unnoticed.

So, I guess that's my story. Looking forward, wouldn't it have been nice to have the child born inside my inn? I could put up a sign saying, "Jesus slept here!" I would never have an empty room. Alas, this is not to be. And I suspect all who listen will like the story just as it is. But for me, well, it is a lost opportunity, for sure!

MARY: I am Christmas. I am Mary. I must confess, I am certainly frightened by all that is going on. At the same time, if I understand correctly, I am greatly honored. I am soon to give birth to a child whose significance I simply cannot understand. Just yesterday it seems, I was just a young Jewish girl, pledged to be married to Joseph. Today, here I am about to become a mother. The mystery of it all, I cannot explain.

But God is soon to do a great work. It was revealed to me—and to my understanding, to Joseph as well—that God is ready to fulfill his promises found in the writings of the prophets of old. And he has chosen me, insignificant though I might be, to play a role in this magnificent drama. This is so hard for me to comprehend. But this is what is now taking place, here in Bethlehem, in this stable, on this night.

Let me ask you a question. If God would choose one like me for this incredible work, could he not choose you as well? Is there something that needs to be done in his kingdom that you can do? It doesn't take courage or greatness to be used by God. It only takes a willingness to be the instrument of his work. Think about what I say. Oh! I think the baby is about to arrive! I had better be going! The birth of my child is going to be wonderful news, don't you concur?

THE STAR: I am Christmas. I am the star that appeared in the east. We stars have been around for a long, long time, since the beginning of time. We provide light and direction for those who wish to journey at night. But I am a special star. My light points to a stable in Bethlehem. I illuminate the way for those who wish to see the newborn infant they call the Christ child. My light is for all who journey, whether they are kings or commoners.

And this Christ child—I really like this—he, I am told, will be called "the Light of the World!" He sounds like a real star to me! He will brighten the lives of those who live in darkness. He will illumine the path of those who earnestly seek to find their way to the love and the light of God. So you see, I am a star who on this night is in excellent company. I have been chosen to guide so many to the one who will become the brightest light of all time.

THE SHEPHERDS IN THE FIELD: We are Christmas. We are the shepherds in the field. We are watching our flock tonight, as we do most every night. Ours is usually not a difficult or challenging work. But it is important. We are a dignified people. We are common, ordinary folk who have performed our task for generations with little or no change. We ask you, how hard is it to keep an eye on a bunch of sheep?

We are part of those who are called "the people of the land." The religious leaders of Judah, especially the Pharisees, they despise us. They turn their noses in the air and look down upon us. We are not good enough for them. But listen closely: we are good enough for God. And this child, he came into the world for all mankind, including the poor and the common people, the socially and religiously despised, the rejected and the weak, the rich and the not-so-rich, the princes and the paupers. This child, when he becomes a man, he will watch over all of us, protect us, and care for us as no one else could ever do. When we stray from the fold (that's shepherd-speak), he will seek us until he finds us and will bring us back to shelter, safe and sound.

You know what we shepherds think? We think he should be called "the Good Shepherd." Certainly no name given to him could ever say more about God's concern and compassion for all of us. "The Good Shepherd." That's a good title, don't you agree?

THE THREE WISE MEN: We are Christmas. We are the three wise men. We are students of the stars. We will travel many miles in order to honor the newborn child. We are royalty from the Orient, and we are convinced the birth of this infant will have meaning for all humankind.

We carry with us special gifts for the child: gold, frankincense, and myrrh. Our gifts symbolize his royalty, his divinity, and his humanity. The last gift, myrrh, is used to embalm a dead body. It reminds us of the time when this child will lay down his life so others may receive life from God.

Like we wise men, this child is also royalty. He will be called the Prince of Peace, as prophesied by Isaiah of old. He will be the King of Kings. But intriguingly, his kingdom will not be of this world. No, his kingdom will be found in the hearts of men, women, and children, who acknowledge his rule. And his kingdom will not be ruled by power and violence, like those of Herod and other earthly kings. His kingdom will be ruled by love.

Well, the journey is long. There is no time to waste. My friends and I must be on our way. The Christ child awaits us. As we seek him, perhaps you should as well?

HEROD THE GREAT: I am Herod. Some call me Herod the Great; that's fine by me. I am also known as the King of the Jews—at least that's my role under Rome. My people ought to love me.

I rebuilt and added to the temple. I built an incredible harbor at Caesarea. I keep the peace. Rome likes its rulers to keep the peace! So what if I raise the people's taxes? And just because I have executed some of my own family (and probably will do in a few more before I am through) I am neither loved nor appreciated. What do these people want?

Oh, well. So, the others who have spoken before me began by saying, "I am Christmas." Well, I suppose I could also state that. There are those who might identify with me during this season. But you won't find me waxing eloquent about how wonderful this newborn infant is.

For you see, some say my jealousy of this child reflects the insecurity of those in this world who are not at peace with themselves or with others. I am like those who hold on to temporal things but are unable or unwilling to grasp things eternal. I am a king with earthly power and political authority, yet, as you know, I am threatened by the birth of a child. So what if I am jealous, suspicious, and weak? Still, that which I seek the most—peace of mind, contentment, hope, respect, and a life that has meaning—others say this can be found in the child.

But I cannot see this. And when I am dead and gone, all the gains and all the glory of this world that I have achieved will mean absolutely nothing. Too many will, like me, fail to understand the significance of this child. Too many will be concerned about the things of this world and will miss God's great gift to mankind.

I know what I'll do. I'll issue orders to have all of the infants in my kingdom eliminated. Maybe this will rid me of this child. Yes, I am Herod the Great! And no one seems to like me!

NARRATOR OR PASTOR: I am Christmas. I have told you who I am in terms of people and places in the Bible. Now, let me try and tell you what I mean for ordinary people like you. I am Christmas, the day you celebrate the birth of Jesus, the Christ and the Savior of mankind. I am redemption for those who are separated from God. I am the story of salvation for all who will seek God through his Son, the one whose birth you honor on this day. I am joy in a world of sorrow. I am peace to men and women of goodwill. I am love in a world of hatred. I bring unity in a divided world. I am light in a world of darkness. I am hope for all who despair. I am the celebration of God's greatest gift to the world— yes, a world that includes even you.

But the most important question I can ask is this: "What am I to you?" A tree decorated with tinsel, twinkling lights, brightly colored bulbs, and a variety of ornaments? Beautifully wrapped packages tied with bows and ribbons? Family and friends gathered around a table covered with ham or turkey and all the trimmings?

All of these things bring joy and happiness to you. They all have an important place in your lives. But when the tree has been taken down, when the decorations have been stored for another year, when the torn wrappings and broken ribbons have been discarded, when the table has been cleared and the dishes washed and put away, and when the friends and relatives have gone home, may you never be embarrassed to say, "Despite all the glitter and sparkle, a star still shines over this place, where the celebration of the birth of God's Son is the most important event of the season. In the midst of all our loved ones, the supreme visitor is still the one who came to shepherds and kings, and to each and every one of us as well."

All the gifts given and all the gifts received during this time are of little value when compared with the great gift of God to you. He has given you himself in the form of a child. And when this child, his Son, became a man, he offered to you the greatest gift a man, woman, or child could ever receive: the gift of salvation. And he purchased this gift by paying the highest price any man could pay. He gave his life in order to give life to each and every one of you. To know this, to believe this, and to live in accord with this—this is to know the true meaning of Christmas.

I am Christmas. I am a time of giving by God and a time of receiving for each of you. God has a gift for you on this Christmas Day. He sent it to you a long time ago. It's not a free gift, but you can't buy it. However, God purchased it long ago with the sacrificed life of his Son. The gift is the offer of salvation. If you have never received this gift, will you accept it today and make this the best Christmas ever?

If you have accepted this gift, will you commit yourself to making Christ central, not just on Christmas Day, but on each day of the year? Will you commit yourself to sharing the gift of God with others in the way you live and serve and care? Will you begin right now by joining all of these others who came to visit and know the Christ child who came so long ago on the first Christmas Day?

RESPONSIVE READING: "WE ARE CHRISTMAS"

NARRATOR OR PASTOR: I am Christmas. I am a child of God. I am love and peace and hope. And so are you, if you know and understand and accept this great gift of God to all the world, which you celebrate on this Christmas Day.

PEOPLE: We are Christmas!

NARRATOR OR PASTOR: We are Christmas!

PEOPLE: We are Christmas!

NARRATOR OR PASTOR: We all are children of God who give witness to the Christ child. We reflect his light in a darkened world.

PEOPLE: We are Christmas!

NARRATOR OR PASTOR: We sing of his joy when surrounded by sorrow and grief. We anticipate his hope for all who are hopeless. We share his gift to those who are in spiritual and physical need. We convey his love in an angry and volatile world. We are the spirit of Christmas for this generation.

PEOPLE: We are Christmas!

NARRATOR OR PASTOR: We are Christmas and we rejoice in God's grace, not just on this day but every day.

ALL: We are Christmas! We are light! We are joy! We are hope! We say again for all to hear, we are Christmas!

ALL SING: "Go Tell It on the Mountain" chorus.

NARRATOR OR PASTOR: A Christmas benediction: "Father, the Christmas season will soon be over. But it never ends. Your love continues to be manifest anew, and it will never cease. The joy, the peace, the hope made known in the Christ child will continue through the generations.

"So, on this Christmas Day, let us rejoice with the ages; let us sing the carols of good tidings for all, and let us live anew the meaning and the message of the Christmas story. Go in peace into the world. Amen."

DRAMATIC READING 2: VOICES FROM THE PASSION WEEK

TEXT:

Matthew 21:1-9 – When they had come near Jerusalem and had reached Bethphage, at the Mount of Olives, Jesus sent two disciples, saying to them, "Go into the village ahead of you, and immediately you will find a donkey tied, and a colt with her; untie them and bring them to me. If anyone says anything to you, just say this, 'The Lord needs them.' And he will send them immediately." This took place to fulfill what had been spoken through the prophet, saying,

"Tell the daughter of Zion, 'Look, your king is coming to you, humble, and mounted on a donkey, and on a colt, the foal of a donkey.'"

The disciples went and did as Jesus had directed them; they brought the donkey and the colt, and put their cloaks on them, and he sat on them. A huge crowd spread their cloaks on the road, and others cut branches from the trees and spread them on the road. The crowds that went ahead of him and that followed were shouting,

"Hosanna to the Son of David!"

"Blessed is he who comes in the name of the Lord!"

"Hosanna in the highest heaven!"

VOICES FROM THE PASSION WEEK

NARRATOR: Jesus's ministry was very brief; three short years. Little is known of his life prior to his baptism by John the Baptist in the Jordan River. He wrote no books. He was never elected to public office. He pastored no church. He never taught at a university or seminary. He never served as a missionary in a distant land.

Jesus, therefore, depended upon a small group of followers the New Testament calls apostles and disciples to continue his message and movement. Events during the last week of his earthly ministry initially gave no hint of a promising future for this limited band of believers. Had his followers not remained faithful and given witness to his life, ministry and teachings, there would have been no church and no New Testament. And we would not be gathered here.

Today we are going to look at the last week in the earthly ministry of Jesus, which we call the Passion Week, and which culminates in the resurrection. We will view important events through the eyes and the stories of some of those who encountered this prophet from Galilee, and even use our imagination a little to create a couple of characters to help us better comprehend the events of these significant days. Hopefully, we will better understand and appreciate the one we know as Jesus. We begin with events prior to the entry of Jesus into Jerusalem on the Sunday before the resurrection.

MARY: Hello, my name is Mary. Welcome to our home here on the Mount of Olives in Bethany. My family and I, including my sister Martha and our brother Lazarus, have lived here for a long, long time. As followers of Jesus, Martha and I are not as well-known as the brothers in the New Testament, such as James and John, or Peter and Andrew. But in our own way, we two siblings make an important contribution to the story of Jesus. We represent two different kinds of people, each cherishing her friendship with him.

This past week is special, for we had an unusual number of visitors stop in. Jesus and several of his close followers arrived for observance of the Passover and remained here for several days, awaiting this important celebration. But there appeared to be more in the air than simply this historic Jewish festival. There was an atmosphere of anticipation, of hope, of fulfillment. Something important was beginning to happen. I sensed it. And Jesus was at the center of it all.

Martha is a doer. She spends most of her time preparing meals and making her guests comfortable, making sure everything is in order. What she does is important; don't get me wrong. We really need the "Marthas" of this world. But we two sisters are quite different. She's a doer; I'm a dreamer! I see beyond what is on the surface. I look for meaning when others don't seem to be concerned.

Let me share with you an example of what I am trying to say. I have followed the life of Jesus closely during the past few years. He is an amazing teacher! There are so many stories about him. He has a reputation for healing the sick and the infirm. There are stories about how he restored the dead back to life. Remember the one about how he raised my brother Lazarus? For many, including myself, Jesus is the long-awaited Messiah. He is the prophet promised in our scared writings. I truly believe this! And I know many, many people are looking for him to do something significant, something dramatic, during the days ahead.

I say all of this to tell you about something that happened a few days ago. Following supper, I took a large jar of precious (and expensive) anointing oil and poured it on the feet of Jesus. I wiped the oil with my hair and the fragrance of the perfume seemed to fill the entire house. Judas, one of his followers—and one I worry about possibly betraying him—criticized me for wasting precious ointment which could have been sold and the money used to help the poor. Rumors are he may be a thief and probably is not really interested in helping the poor. I shouldn't be spreading rumors, but I didn't like his accusing me.

But Jesus defended me and interpreted what I had done as symbolic of preparing his body for burial. That was quite surprising, and disturbing, actually at the same time. But the events of the following days made what he was saying clear. I didn't understand everything that was happening, but I did know, I did believe, he was someone special, someone whose life and ministry would make a great difference in the days and years to come. Do you understand what I am saying? I believe that for all of us who are his followers, we will continue to learn and grow in our understanding of who he is, what he is doing, and how his life and ministry are so relevant for our relationships with each other, and with God.

But there are other stories to be told, so I will say no more except for one last thing: the small role I am playing in this drama is personal to me and my understanding of the place of Jesus in history. And now, I want to point you from Bethany to the historic city of Jerusalem, where much of the story of Jesus unfolded. But first, here's my sister.

MARTHA: Hello, my name is Martha. And yes, I am the sister of Mary. We are not exactly identical twins! In fact, we are not twins at all, just sisters. Like Mary indicated, she is a dreamer. Me? I am simply a doer. She is outgoing; I am quiet. People enjoy being around her, but they hardly notice me. And I like it like that!

What I do and how I do it is important. When people are hungry, I prepare meals and feed them. When the followers of Jesus need a place to relax and rest, I prepare a place for them. When they need someone to run an errand, I am the one they turn to.

Some may think that I am not a great thinker, but I am just reserved in speaking openly. And I may not appear to be visionary, but if you want something done, well, I am the right person to ask. I will get it done, and on time. I am dependable. If I say I will do something, I will do it. I see myself as a doer, not a dreamer.

In fact, I believe the law of common sense is the best law there is. That's all I depend upon, so I don't focus much on the Jewish Law. And this is one of things I like about Jesus: he gives you the freedom to do what is right. He really cares about people much more than he cares about rules and regulations for them. What he says and what he does are for the benefit of the people. I heard him say that the Sabbath was made for us, not the other way around. That makes sense. I heard what he said in his sermon on the mountainside in Galilee. He emphasized our attitudes and our motives as the basis for our actions, not simply following legalistic demands.

He sees the good in tax collectors, fishermen, and shepherds! Why, he even sees the good in Samaritans and gentiles. Look at some of the people who hang around him: common, ordinary folk. He does not look down upon women, as so many of the religious leaders do; rather, he encourages and affirms those he encounters.

So I know Jesus likes people like me, the doers of this world, the dependable, ordinary, hard-working people, not just the big-idea people. As followers of Jesus, my sister and I are two sides of the same coin. We both appreciate each other and what the other brings to the table! *Brings to the table*—now that is something with which I can identify. I have to go. Someone is calling for more bread and wine. I wonder who this is who is getting ready to speak. Rather strange looking, I must say.

JERUSALEM: Good morning! I must warn you, you are going to have to use your creative imagination with me. You see, all the other characters in this story are people. But not me! I am a city, and my story is very important to the story of Jesus.

More precisely, I am the ancient city of Jerusalem. For centuries I have been the spiritual and political capital of the Jewish people. Many outside invaders have assaulted me throughout my existence. For example, about nine hundred years ago Shishak, the Egyptian pharaoh, invaded Judah and placed me under siege. He carried off treasures from the temple when I surrendered. About six hundred years ago, the Babylonians under Nebuchadnezzar captured me and destroyed my walls. He razed Solomon's sacred temple to the ground. Then, the Babylonians carried my leading citizens into exile to Babylon, one of several Babylonian deportations. A generation or so later, Cyrus, a Persian ruler, conquered the Babylonians. He allowed the Jews who chose to do so to come back to me. He also appointed Nehemiah as governor to rebuild my walls for my protection.

In the second century BC, a Greek ruler from Syria named Antiochus IV began to call himself "Epiphanes," which means "the Manifest God." Not exactly a humble designation. In a play on words, many Jews derisively called him "Epimanes," which means "the Insane One." Obviously, he was unpopular in Palestine. Why? Because around 168 BC, he invaded me, established worship to Zeus in my rebuilt temple, and sacrificed a sow upon the great altar to the Lord! Want to stir up the locals? Then sacrifice a pig on the great altar to the Lord in the temple! The Jews revolted. Eventually I and the country were freed by the Maccabees, a Jewish group led by a man named Judas whose friends called him the "Maccabean," or the "Hammerer." He was my hero!

Dark days often come my way. I endure hard times over and over again, but I always rise up to overcome my next challenge. Now, although under Roman rule, my people once more seek God's intervention for my freedom and his glory.

Allow me to set the current scene for you. It is the time of the Hebrew Passover. Celebrants are arriving from all over the Roman Empire. They are flocking through my gates by the thousands, reminded of God's deliverance from Egypt during the time of the exodus more than a millennium ago. These pilgrims are seeking a similar deliverance from the power of the Romans.

So, on this Sunday there seems to be a special energy present. A young prophet from Nazareth, I hear his name is Jesus, enters my gates. A clamorous throng is gathering. Many believe this prophet is the long-awaited Messiah, God's anointed one. They believe he will deliver the Hebrew people from foreign oppression once more and will establish God's kingdom within my ancient walls once again.

This Galilean from Nazareth comes to me riding a donkey, that lowly beast of burden. Some interpret this act as a fulfillment of a Hebrew prophecy from Zechariah, who wrote of a humble king who enters the city riding on a lowly beast of burden. People are throwing leafy branches and palm leaves in his path. On your calendar, this day is called "Palm Sunday." The branches are much more than just a natural carpet to soften the path for this prophet: they symbolize Jewish nationalism. Many of those gathered along this path identify this prophet as a political and military leader who will restore the nation of Israel to her former greatness and overthrow oppressive foreign rulers (you know who I am talking about: Caesar). Jesus will restore the glory of God's people—and my glory as well. But I mentioned that, didn't I?

This week I will be the setting of a unique drama. Events of monumental importance will occur, which will change the world. No ordinary person could possibly predict what is about to happen. I am Jerusalem, and once again all eyes will be upon me—and upon this prophet from Nazareth.

ZECHARIAH, A BOY: Hey there and good morning! I'm Zechariah. My parents like the Hebrew prophets a lot, so they named me after one of them. But my friends, well they just call me Zack. I love living in Jerusalem. So much goes on in this town! Visitors are always showing up for some religious holiday, plus all those here for everyday business. It's fun watching them and talking to them when I get a chance. Some of them come from other places in Palestine. Some come all of the way from Rome or from some other big cities in the Roman Empire, like Alexandria, Ephesus, and Antioch. I dream of seeing all these places someday. Imagine what you could learn! Yep, I love living in Jerusalem!

Let me tell you what I saw last Sunday. It was really great! I was so excited. I had so much fun! This place was really alive—and why? This young fellow from Nazareth arrived. At least that's what people were saying. I've always wanted to go to Nazareth. Have you ever been there? They said his name was Jesus. I heard someone say he was a prophet. Not like these moneychangers in the temple—you know their kind. When they talk of "profit," well, they mean your money in their pockets.

Anyway, I've never seen or heard a real prophet, unless this Jesus really is one. Have you ever seen a prophet? I guess he looked like a prophet. He dressed like everybody else, nothing fancy about him. And he came riding into town on a donkey—a donkey mind you. A donkey! That sounds to me like something a prophet would ride, don't you think? Well, back to what I was telling you about last Sunday.

There was this rabbi-looking guy who told me Zechariah—the prophet, not me—that rabbi said this Jesus is fulfilling one of Zechariah's prophecies that said this guy from God was going to enter Jerusalem in peace, riding this lowly beast of burden. Riding this donkey. I don't know, but it sounds good to me. I mean how many prophets are going to be riding into Jerusalem on a donkey these days?

And, boy, after he got into Jerusalem did it get wild. All these people were shouting "Hosanna!"—you know, "God save us!" They were calling Jesus a king. I've never seen a king before, have you? And they were throwing down palm branches in front of him. I got caught up in it and was so excited that I started yelling and running and jumping up to see him! And I don't even know why!

And do you know what happened next? He paused and looked me straight in the eye, like I was the only one there in this huge crowd. And then he smiled at me. He had, how shall I put it...he had warm, kind, caring eyes. They sparkled! And then he patted me on the head and rode on. I think I like him a lot! And then he disappeared, and so did the crowd. But it sure was fun while it lasted!! Wow!

Uh oh, here comes Simeon the money changer on his way to the temple to make his profit and steal cash from the people. He doesn't like us kids hanging around and causing a stir. I better run for it. See you later! Hey Simeon, na-na-na-na-na. Catch me if you can!!

[He laughs as he goes off.]

SIMEON, THE MONEYCHANGER: Brats! Hey kid, your father is a gentile! Get outta here! Oh, good morning. I am Simeon. I am a money exchanger here in the temple. Are you here for the Passover? Festivals like Passover are really great for business. Travelers from all over the Roman Empire come to Jerusalem to celebrate the Passover and the Feast of Unleavened Bread. They see this as a time for remembering. I see it as an opportunity—to cash in on the presence of these visitors. You surely know my slogan: "It pays to be religious."

Look, here's the way things work. When visitors come to the temple to buy sacrificial animals, they have to pay for them in Jewish shekels. The priests won't accept pagan coins to pay for animals that they sacrifice in the Jewish temple, and why should they? And, thanks to me and my cohorts, there's no need to pay for clean animals with unclean coins. The priests make sure all sacrificial laws are enforced, and we give them a little kickback for their trouble. As currency changers we provide visitors who need to convert their foreign currency into Jewish money with an important service—for a price, of course. A very hefty fee. They are a "captive audience," so to speak.

But we money changers are not nearly as bad as the sellers of the sacrificial animals. Those "merchants" have a deal with the priests, which is even more lucrative than the one the priests have with us money exchangers. Many pilgrims bring their own animals for sacrifice, so they don't have to buy them here. There is quite a markup when you buy locally.

But their animals—doves and lambs, for example—have to be perfect and approved by the priests. And the priests usually find some flaw which makes the visitors' animals unsuitable. So the visitors are forced to buy one of the "certified animals" from the vendors, which of course have the stamp of priestly approval on them. I have heard—not saying it is true—the priests then take some of the animals that have not been accepted and channel them to the vendors as approved sacrifices, who then sell these animals to other pilgrims. Quite a lucrative – and I might add – corrupt system.

But let me tell you what happened a few days ago. This fellow from Nazareth—I think his name is Jesus—has developed quite a reputation, but if you ask me, he is nothing more than a trouble-maker. Some say he is a prophet. I say he hurts *my* profit. Some call him a "king." He created quite a stir when he came into Jerusalem a day or two ago—riding on a donkey! Huh! Not exactly the preferred mode of travel for royals, don't you think?

Anyway, this Jesus shows up here in the courtyard, and let me tell you, he went on an absolute rampage. He turned over our tables and drove out the money exchangers and the sellers of the sacrificial animals with his whip! Man, I hightailed it out of there. I barely escaped with my treasure!

He also quoted from Isaiah and Jeremiah. That's nothing new; people are always citing the prophets as proof texts of their radical views. However, he did sound like a prophet of old, saying the temple was supposed to be a house of prayer but that I and my kind have made it into a den of robbers and thieves. I didn't appreciate his comment identifying me with robbers and thieves. Would you? Look, I'm just trying to make an honest living—well, at least a living.

I heard he placed a curse on a barren fig tree on his way into the city, saying it symbolized the barrenness of our religious leaders. He may be on to something there? Anyway, after his scene here in the temple, the religious and political leaders turned against him. It appeared they were looking for a way to get this trouble-maker out of their hair. And they will! You can count on it.

I also hear that the chief priests and the elders, the scribes and Pharisees, the Sadducees, and the Herodians—just about any leader who was anybody—kept asking him all kinds of theological and religious questions. They were just trying to trap him. They asked him questions about the resurrected life and relationships, John's authority—you know, the one called "the Baptist,"—paying taxes to Caesar, and which is the greatest commandment. I don't care which commandment is the greatest, but my least favorites are the two about coveting and stealing. Not that I would ever do those things.

Anyway, I don't care much for theology. I can't understand it; can you? Well, Jesus was a real thorn in the flesh for all of them. One needs to avoid making enemies of people who have so much authority and power, believe you me. But the guy is a real deep thinker, sort of a teacher. He answered every one of their questions. He revealed a great deal of intelligence and wisdom. In fact, he even asked a question of his own about the Messiah, which they could not even come close to answering or understanding. Not that it made much sense to me either, but like I said, I'm not much of a theologian, and I never intend to be one.

Sorry, excuse me, looks like a customer's coming, needing to exchange a few coins. It's been nice to chat with you. Have a good visit, and if you need some cash, you know where to find me. Don't forget this other slogan of mine: "A shekel from me, sets all your sins free!"

[He laughs as he departs.]

JOHN MARK: Good morning! I am John Mark. I am not one of the apostles. My mother is a follower of Jesus, and she influenced me to pay attention to all he taught. My uncle lives on the island of Cyprus, but he is here in Jerusalem right now. We call him Barnabas, a nickname meaning "Son of Encouragement." He is a dedicated Jew but he is also open to new ideas, like many of those Jews who live outside of Palestine. [He cups his hand over his mouth] He even hangs around with gentiles! He quickly became a follower of Jesus, and that influenced me to follow Jesus too.

I'm much too young to be taken seriously, but I'm a rather inquisitive kind of guy. I like to lurk around, watch what is going on, observe what is happening—and what might happen.

Let me tell you a few things I have noticed and heard. Jesus has this close group of followers called apostles. They are an unusual and diverse group of people: fishermen, tax collectors, common laborers; not the kind of folks you would think could change the world, you know what I mean?

James and John are two brothers who are loyal on the one hand and quite ambitious on the other. Once when Jesus was talking about his kingdom, they got him to one side and asked if they could sit on either side of his throne. They wanted to be where the power is. But I always thought Jesus was not really talking about an earthly kingdom, but something else, kind of a spiritual kingdom. I haven't quite been able to completely figure out what he meant. Do you understand what I'm saying? Anyway, James and John could be rather volatile. I remember them wanting to bring down fire and brimstone on their enemies. That's a good strategy to win people over to your side, right? But I don't think this is the best way to get fired up for Jesus, and it's not exactly consistent with the teachings of Jesus on peace, and love, and hope.

Let me tell you about Simon Peter. His brother, Andrew, is also a close follower of Jesus. Peter is actually a nickname; we Jews seem to like nicknames. Nicknames can tell you a lot about a person. Peter means "Rock." In many ways Peter is a rock, as solid a supporter of Jesus as you can find. He is enthusiastic and boisterous; he frequently sticks his foot in his mouth. But when he is humbled, he learns from it. I think this will be important for him in the work he will do later.

During the time of Passover, Jesus had a special fellowship meal with his followers. It was similar to the Passover but also a bit different. He broke bread and poured out wine to symbolize what he said would soon take place. It's the kind of event that those who were there will still talk about years later.

Jesus also predicted his followers would betray him. Well, Peter boasted that though all the others might betray Jesus, he never would. It's easy to boast about what you *would* do, don't you agree? But when push comes to shove, well...

Jesus told Peter that before the sun came up the next day, Peter would deny him three times. I am certain Peter found this to be preposterous! At least until he heard the rooster crowing. All the others also joined in and pledged their support no matter what happened. Boy, were they wrong.

I was close by and heard Jesus also tell Peter that he would return to follow him again, and Jesus instructed him at that time to strengthen the others. What Jesus said didn't make a lot of sense at the time, but I can see Peter as a leader of the followers of Jesus. Like I said, I like Peter. And he tells funny stories, often about himself. Maybe someday I can work with him.

Following the fellowship meal, Jesus and his friends made their way to a nearby garden, a place called Gethsemane on the Mount of Olives. As he went deeper into the garden, some of the group stayed at the entrance to watch. Peter, James, and John went a ways further. They were also supposed to keep watch, but they fell asleep. Jesus went deeper into the garden to pray.

As he finished praying, a mob showed up and chaos broke out. The words of Jesus predicting he would be betrayed came true. Judas Iscariot, another apostle, had betrayed Jesus. I never really liked Judas; he seemed sneaky and was always raising questions inconsistent with what Jesus was saying. I think he may have wanted Jesus to be a political or military leader and foment a rebellion against Rome instead of being a religious leader. Maybe this explains what would soon happen. What do you think?

Well, Judas was the treasurer for the group, even though some thought he was a thief! Apparently, he had cut a deal with the religious leaders: for thirty pieces of silver he would lead this mob to Jesus. He was there when a bunch of ruffians confronted Jesus in the garden that night. He identified him with a kiss on the cheek, and they arrested Jesus. Peter drew a sword, and the other apostles initially responded. But in the end, they all fled off into the night.

Bet you wonder how I know all this! Well, I watched the whole thing. I sneaked out of my home wrapped in my bed sheet. I was in a big hurry to run and catch the group when they left my mother's house and didn't take time to get dressed. When things got out of hand in the garden, one of the guards grabbed my sheet, but I escaped, "streaking," as some say in your genera- tion, into the night. Not exactly my finest hour, but in hindsight, a rather amusing story in the midst of a terrifying moment. Well, perhaps some time later on I can write down these and other things related to the life and ministry of Jesus. Hopefully, the sto- ry will be a gospel, or "good news," for those who read it. What do you think? Would there be a need for a book like this? Well, I have to run. I'm always running off somewhere. But this time I am dressed. Aren't we all glad?

CAIAPHAS, THE HIGH PRIEST: My name is Caiaphas. I am the high priest, the most important office in Judaism these days. The position of the high priesthood is carefully controlled by just a few families. For example, not only did my father-in-law Annas serve as high priest, but so did six of his sons. After he ran out of sons, he maneuvered to have me, his son-in-law, elected to the office.

As high priest I have enormous political power and unquestioned religious authority, more than any other person in Judea. But I also have a lot of responsibility, and Rome is always looking over my shoulder. I and my fellow members of the Sanhedrin, the seventy-member ruling council of the Jews, are expected to take care of the needs of the Jewish people. We also are given the responsibility by Rome of keeping the peace, making sure no person or group destabilizes Judea in any way. Rome holds us accountable for preventing any revolutionary from coming in here and upsetting the order of things. We simply cannot allow this! Do you understand what I am saying?

This is the reason why this Jesus fellow from Nazareth is so disturbing to us. He has been stirring up trouble for a while. Suddenly he shows up here in Jerusalem. Not only did he attack our leaders, including those of us in the Sanhedrin, but did you hear about the scene in the temple? Things were getting out of hand. We had to do something. We were responsible for putting an end to this travesty. So we arrested him.

Annas met with Jesus. I did tell you Annas is my father-in-law, didn't I? He continues to exert a lot of power. Then this Jesus was brought before me. I interrogated him, as did the Sanhedrin. We concluded that we needed to get rid of him. A charge of blasphemy would do it, but Rome won't let us Jews execute people. Rome wants that authority for herself. So, we changed the single charge to multiple ones founded on political issues: treason, sedition, insurrection, and threatening to overthrow Rome. I think we can depend on Pilate to do what needs to be done, don't you? Well, well, here he comes. He wants to speak.

PONTIUS PILATE, THE ROMAN PROCURATOR: My name is Pontius Pilate. I am the Roman procurator. I collect taxes, but the office has grown beyond tax collecting in power and responsibility. In effect, I am now the governor of Judea. I am sure you know the events that brought this Galilean Jew before me. I saw no reason to punish him; this was nothing more than a Jewish religious squabble. But this is one of the burdens of my office, so I had to deal with it.

I asked this Jesus several questions, but he was not cooperative. I asked him if he was the "King of the Jews." If he was, he was a pretty pathetic figure to carry such a title! He simply replied that this was what I was saying. Not exactly a definitive answer.

I consulted with Herod Antipas, not one of my favorite people, but he is the ruler or king over Galilee and this Jesus was a Galilean, so it seemed appropriate. And, wouldn't you know it, Herod left it up to me! I decided to get Jesus released from custody. We had two robbers and a revolutionary awaiting execution, so I offered the people the choice to set one prisoner free, knowing it would be Jesus rather than the revolutionary (named Barabbas) or one of the robbers. Pretty clever on my part, wouldn't you say?

I must say I was stunned when the crowd selected Barabbas, but not as surprised as Barabbas, I'm sure. But the crowd, at the instigation of the religious leaders, demanded Jesus be crucified. This was not what I wanted! But my hands were tied. What could I do? So I delivered Jesus to the soldiers to be crucified. I understand they mocked him, scourged him, and then took him out to be crucified with the two robbers. I assume that this was end of the story—at least I think so. I washed my hands of the whole matter. At least Rome can't be on my back over this radical "King of the Jews!"

MARY MAGDALENE: Hello. I am Mary Magdalene. I am from a small village on the western shore of the Sea of Galilee. I first met Jesus when he was preaching and teaching in the area. He attracted many followers, including myself. He gave us hearers hope for the first time in a long time. He was a prophet if I ever saw one.

Jesus accepted me as a friend, like he has for so many of us common, hard-working people in Galilee. I count myself among those who believe he is the one promised to us in the Scriptures and the one who will be God's agent of redemption, of salvation for the people. This servant is described as a light to the nations and the one who fulfills the teachings of many of the Hebrew prophets.

But things have gotten really confusing, even disappointing, in the last several days. I won't retell the stories of all the events that have happened since Jesus arrived in Jerusalem. But I will tell you I was not expecting him to be arrested and put to death. None of us were! We were shattered!

Crucifixion is a horrible punishment, even more so for one who does not deserve a fate like that. But it happened. We had no time to grieve. We had to move rapidly to prepare his body for burial before the Sabbath began at sundown on that Friday.

A few members of the Sanhedrin, the Jewish ruling council, were followers of Jesus. They responded quickly to help us. Nicodemus is one. You remember him: the one who visited Jesus at night. Jesus told him that God loved the word so much that he was willing to give up his Son in order to give eternal life to all who would follow him. It is confusing, but I'm wondering if, in all the events of the last few days, God may be fulfilling these words of Jesus. What is significant at this moment is that Nicodemus provided us with the spices and oils necessary to prepare the body of Jesus for burial. I am certain he will be criticized by other members of the Sanhedrin for doing this, but that doesn't seem to bother him. He is without question a genuinely good man.

Another concern was where to place the body. Again, a member of the Sanhedrin stepped forward. Joseph of Arimathea, who apparently is also a follower of Jesus, provided a newly cut tomb, which is close by. He is both kind and courageous in doing this for us and for Jesus.

So, I and a few friends, namely Mary the mother of James and Joseph, along with Joanna and Salome, worked quickly to prepare the body and place it in the tomb. Soldiers then rolled a stone over the entrance.

Now, for the first time, we can pause and reflect on all that has happened. I ask you, does the story end here? Why did these events take place? Did Jesus pose a genuine threat to the religious establishment and the Roman rulers, so they had to get rid of him? Will the story conclude with memories of a man who was an outstanding teacher and a prophet who helped us to believe and dream, but who in the end simply did not fulfill his promises because of Roman execution? Somehow, I don't believe it is over. I still have hope; I still believe. But now what happens to those of us who believe in him? The stone sealing the entrance to the tomb seems so final.

Well, I must go and meet with the others. We have a lot to talk about, a lot to figure out. My friends and I are coming back on Sunday morning. The Sabbath will be over, and there is still more to do for the final preparation of his body. We didn't have time to do everything we wanted on Friday, but on Sunday we can pay true homage to our friend.

Who knows, maybe come Sunday morning we can take the time to rekindle our hopes and dreams. Maybe, somehow, some way, God will turn this tragedy into a victory for we who still believe that Jesus came from God for a special purpose. Maybe the story is not over. Maybe it is just beginning! Or maybe I am just a dreamer? What do you think? Is there more to come? Would you like to join us Sunday morning? Maybe we will all be in for a big surprise? Besides, you know, we'll need plenty of help to roll the heavy stone away.

NARRATOR: For we twenty-first century believers, the story is not over. Defeat will end in victory. Death will result in life. Soon we will celebrate the resurrection, the event which gives meaning and understanding to all the events of the Passion Week. The story continues with a message of rejoicing, hope, and anticipation. There is indeed good news for those of us who are followers of Jesus.

DRAMATIC READING 3: MY NAME IS BAPTIST BUT MY FRIENDS CALL ME LIBERTY

<u>TEXTS:</u>

2 Corinthians 3:17 – Now the Lord is the Spirit, and where the Spirit of the Lord is, there is freedom.

Galatians 5:1 – It is for freedom that Christ has set us free. Stand firm, then, and do not let yourselves be burdened again by a yoke of slavery.

Galatians 5:13 – You, my brothers and sisters, were called to be free. But do not use your freedom to indulge the flesh; rather, serve one another humbly in love.

<u>INTRODUCTION:</u>

We gather today to celebrate one of the most significant historical events in the establishment of our nation. On July 4 we celebrate independence, and freedom, and democracy. We celebrate the anniversary of the Declaration of Independence, a historical document penned by Thomas Jefferson and affirmed by a group of courageous revolutionaries opposed to British rule. Fireworks will explode loudly and brightly as they fill the night sky. Our celebrations will be so joyous and so noisy one might conclude we invented liberty. But that is far from the case. So, let me share with you a story of liberty that began long before your ancestors rebelled against the British. Today I have invited four Baptist freedom lovers whose courage and conviction impacted the generations that followed them through the pages of history right up to the doorstep of the contemporary generation. But first let me begin by introducing myself.

MY NAME IS BAPTIST – BUT MY FRIENDS CALL ME LIBERTY!
NARRATOR: Good morning. Some four hundred-plus years ago, in late 1608 or early 1609, we Baptists originated because of intolerance and persecution resulting from a union of church and state. The establishment was the Church of England, and the state was the nation of England. The king at the time was James I. You know him: the one whose name is identified with the long-standing translation of the Bible, the King James Version, which appeared in 1611, just a few years after the beginning of the people called Baptists.

King James promised to "harry out of the land" those who dissented against his church. This was no idle threat. He carried out his promise. A group of English Separatists fled on a ship to Amsterdam, Holland. The Dutch had suffered greatly during the Inquisition, so they were sensitive to those facing religious persecution. Pastor John Smyth led the group. Thomas Helwys, a wealthy businessman, financed the journey of the church into exile. Not much later, he would lead a minority of the church to continue the heritage of this group, following a split with Smyth that resulted from a division in this first "Baptist" church.

Now, allow me to present to you several excellent examples of Baptists who understood the importance of liberty like few others during their times. They will introduce themselves and tell you their stories, respectively. Here comes the first one now.

JOHN SMYTH: Good morning. My name is John Smyth, but my friends call me "Liberty." I was born in the 1500s. I grew up in the Church of England but became an English Separatist. As Separatists we believed the local congregation was given all authority under Christ, rather than a group of high-minded, high-ranking bishops. I and my church were driven into exile to Amsterdam. After a thorough search of the Scriptures, I reached the conclusion that a church should be comprised of baptized believers. What did I do? I baptized myself by affusion, where you pour a hand or cup of water over the head. Then I baptized in the same manner all the rest of the church members. By this action we established the first Baptist church ("Baptist" is the nickname our opponents called us at a later time, I might add).

Because my fellow believers and I faced religious intolerance, in 1609 I became one of the first Englishmen to call for toleration of all Christians! In fact, I may have been the first person to make this plea. Other English dissenters prior to this time called for toleration by the Church of England and by the state, but they only wanted it for themselves, not others. I went a step further. I insisted that all Christians should be tolerated and not persecuted because of their Christian beliefs. I was calling for religious freedom for all Christians, but I came up short of demanding universal liberty of conscience for everyone.

I need to add that in 1612 I led a majority of my church to seek membership in a group known as the Waterlander Mennonites. I did so because I began to doubt my self-baptism. The Mennonite group practiced believer's baptism. I passed away before being accepted by them, but the others who came with me were eventually received.

Not everyone in my first church joined our efforts to unite with the Mennonites. Thomas Helwys became pastor of the remaining minority, and they continued the tradition of the Baptist movement. During the succeeding years, Helwys became the first and most vocal advocate of freedom of religious conscience for all. Let him tell you his story. Here he comes now.

THOMAS HELWYS: Hello. Thomas Helwys is my name, but my friends know me as "Liberty." I was a member in Smyth's church in Amsterdam, which became the first Baptist congregation. I am a well-to-do businessman and I financed the emigration of the church to Amsterdam. The church split shortly after organizing—proving beyond a shadow of a doubt that we were true Baptists, even if we did not use the name at this time. Those who did not follow Smyth to seek membership with the Waterlander Mennonites chose me as pastor. We considered ourselves the true church following the division. Of course, John Smyth's group did the same.

In 1612 I published a book entitled *The Mystery of Iniquity*. In it, I proved I was a radical, a revolutionary for my day—and perhaps your day as well! I sought much more than toleration. I proposed complete liberty of conscience on matters of religion for all. And I do mean *all*. I stated that "men's religion is betwixt God and themselves." Then I wrote that "whether they be heretikes, Turkes, Jewes, or whatsoever," it is no business of the civil magistrates or the king's representatives to punish anyone for his or her religious convictions. Were you listening carefully? Did you hear what I said? No civil official should punish anyone over religious issues, no matter who they are or what they believe— heretics! Turks or Muslims! Jews! Did I leave anyone out? If so, add "whatsoever!" There, everyone is covered! Many credit me as being the first voice in the English language calling for complete freedom of religion, or universal liberty of conscience in matters of religion. They are right!

Do you think I was wishy-washy, too weak, too compromising, or too tolerant? I was not! I simply believe each person must stand before his or her maker and answer to their God alone. Period! A religious group does not need the support of the state to enforce its beliefs and practices, nor should it have to face a hostile state opposing its beliefs. Remember, God, and only God, determines the validity of your faith. Never forget this!

Furthermore, I was so convinced of my views that I sent a copy of my book to the king. I wonder if King James ever read it? Probably not! In the same year I published my book, I led our church back to England. This was an illegal act, but we were determined to return to our homeland. We settled in a place called Spitalfields, which is across the Thames from London. We were the first Baptist church on English soil. I say to you with the greatest conviction possible, all people must be free to practice their faith in their own country without fear or hostility from the state. Everyone! Everyone!

Do you understand how radical, how revolutionary, my views were in the early seventeenth century? No church had ever survived without government backing. But I opposed the accepted belief that churches could not survive without a union of church and state. My message is relevant everywhere, at all times, whether it is the seventeenth century or the twenty-first century or any century. There are no exceptions to *everywhere*. Let me state this clearly: true religion must be free religion.

And what were the consequences of my actions? I was arrested and thrown into London's notorious Newgate prison, where I died sometime during the next four years. Why? Because I not only believed in liberty, but I chose to practice liberty, even if it cost me my life! And even though I died for my beliefs, my witness lives on, especially on the day when you remember your freedoms! Do not forget how many paid the price for your freedoms, including me. Well, it is time for me to step aside for another voice from the past, a voice from your side of the Atlantic.

ROGER WILLIAMS: My name is Roger Williams, but my friends call me "Liberty." I was an Englishman who migrated to colonial Boston. I soon settled in Salem, where I became the minister at the Congregationalist church in the early 1630s. I soon got into trouble (you knew I had some Baptist blood in me even before I became a "Baptist!") when I criticized the state church. I also rejected the king's claim to ownership of the Indians' land. The civil authorities arrested me, then tried, convicted, and sentenced me to be exiled from the colony. I don't know why, but luckily for me the Massachusetts Bay Colony governor, John Winthrop, warned me before sentencing and I fled for my life. Some friendly Indians gave me shelter and when I was terribly sick that winter, they nursed me back to health. I called my new home Providence Plantations.

In 1639 I met a group of Baptists who were also seeking refuge from the Boston authorities. Those Boston Puritans did not come to the New World to establish religious freedom for all, despite the claims of later generations. I purchased land from the Indians, and we organized the first Baptist church on American soil in that same year. Our church is known today as First Baptist Church of Providence, Rhode Island. Have any of you ever visited this church?

I was a Baptist only a few months before becoming a "Seeker," which I remained for the rest of my life. But you Baptists love to claim me even today. The primary reason for this continued Baptist attitude toward me is my insistence upon complete religious freedom for everyone, even those I didn't particularly like. For example, I did not like the Quakers. They were too emotional, too enthusiastic, too vocal, and too loud. But I defended their right to believe and practice their faith. True freedom is when you can respect and defend the freedom of all others, even when you vehemently disagree with them. Well, so many dissenting groups came to Providence Plantations from the other New England colonies that Governor Winthrop of Massachusetts referred to us Rhode Islanders as "the sewer of New England." Not exactly a compliment!

Rhode Island Colony was granted its charter in 1662. I worked hard at obtaining the charter and was very proud it. It guaranteed religious liberty for all, period: no exceptions, none whatsoever. I sound a lot like that Thomas Helwys character, don't I? And the charter guaranteed the right to vote for all, including women. We were way ahead of others when it came to freedom. Henry C. Vedder, a prominent twentieth century historian of Baptists in America, concluded that Rhode Island was the first state ever established on the principle of religious liberty and separation of church and state, a source of pride for all Baptists!

So, when you think of the Founding Fathers, men like Thomas Jefferson and James Madison, just remember that I laid the foundation a century ahead of them. They get most of the credit, but I laid the foundation! And I not only believed in freedom, I practiced it! Well, there is one other Baptist who wants to speak to you, so I yield the floor.

JOHN LELAND: My name is John Leland—Elder John Leland—but my friends call me "Liberty." I was a Separate Baptist from the Middle Colonies but spent many years in Orange County, Virginia. So much took place during my years in the South: The colonies won their independence. After the failure of the Articles of Confederation, we began to debate a new constitution for the country. The Revolutionary War was won, but establishing a national government was a real challenge!

These days were challenging at times. We Separate Baptists were quite evangelistic and not well-liked by many. On one occasion I was preparing to baptize a woman convert. Her husband was opposed to me baptizing her and came looking for me. He carried a gun and was planning to shoot me! I sent out a detachment of men who detained him while I baptized the woman!

Did you know my fellow Baptists and I made a significant contribution to the Constitution, especially in terms of the Bill of Rights? When a call was sent out to hold a convention in Philadelphia to consider adoption of a constitution for the United States of America, states and counties held elections to select delegates to the convention. We Baptists in Orange County, Virginia, promoted our own candidate. We planned to elect and send our person to vote against the proposed constitution!

You want to know why? Because the proposed constitution had no guarantees of the basic freedoms for which so many of us had fought. For example, religious freedom was not guaranteed! In fact, Article 6 is the only place in the Constitution today that mentions religion. It states there will be "no religious test" to hold federal office. That's it, nothing more. And the Constitution as adopted at the convention didn't even apply to the states, just the federal government. But we Baptists also insisted upon other freedoms: speech, press, assembly, and the right to take our grievances to the government. We Baptists love freedom, fought for freedom in the Revolution, and demanded our freedoms be written into the law of the land.

So, we Baptists weren't going to stand for the shortcomings in the proposed constitution. We selected our candidate and intended to elect him as a delegate from Orange County. We were going to instruct him to go and lead the fight to reject the proposed document. Let me be clear: this was not because we were anti-patriotic. In fact, it was just the opposite. As I stated before, we fought for basic freedoms and we insisted upon those freedoms being guaranteed!

As it happened there was another candidate, James Madison. I know you have heard of him, probably as the fourth president of the United States. Madison met with us, but initially he was not concerned with the lack of guarantees of basic freedoms. He believed they were implied in the proposed constitution. Well, we met with him for several hours. We convinced him that such guarantees were essential to our desires and our support. Let me tell you this, when you get surrounded by a bunch of belligerent Baptists, you can have a change of heart and mind in a hurry. We made our case with passion. When the meeting was over, Madison promised to support constitutional amendments to guarantee our important rights, if we would support him.

We agreed, withdrew our candidate, and promoted Madison's candidacy, and he was elected as a delegate to the constitutional convention in Philadelphia. The convention adopted the Constitution in 1787. Then, at the first meeting of Congress, Madison introduced what you know as the "Bill of Rights," or the first ten amendments to the Constitution of the United States of America.

The First Amendment includes several basic rights. Can you name them? They are freedom of speech, freedom of the press, freedom of assembly, and freedom to address our grievances to our government. But to me and my fellow Baptists, the most important freedom was freedom of religion, and Madison listed it first.

Here's how the First Amendment begins: "Congress shall make no law respecting an establishment or religion, or prohibiting the free exercise thereof." Every Baptist, every Christian, every person of faith, and every citizen, even nonbelievers, should thank us Baptists for our contribution to the Constitution of the United States. The Bill of Rights became law in December of 1791. I encourage you to believe these amendments, to defend them, and to practice them. History teaches us that if we don't, we might just lose them!

Now repeat after me: "Congress shall make no law respecting an establishment of religion, or prohibiting the free exercise thereof." Doesn't this sound great? If it does, don't forget to thank me and my fellow Baptists in Orange County, Virginia! And just call us "Liberty!"

Well, it's time for me to step aside. Here comes another Baptist. In fact, you may recognize him. I hear he has roamed the United States for a number of years now. Here he comes.

NARRATOR: Good morning, my name is Baptist, but my friends call me "Liberty." I am not one person, but many. And I have been around for several hundred years. So much of who I am and what I believe rests upon the foundation laid by these earlier Baptists who came before me. My, how I appreciate all for which they stood, all they accomplished, and all they sacrificed for the most noble of principles, especially the principle of liberty; of freedom.

John Smyth took a big step forward calling for religious liberty for all Christians, not just his group. And Thomas Helwys—one of my favorite heroes of the Baptist faith—truly practiced what he preached, giving his life for his beliefs. No voice is louder than his when it comes to religious liberty for all, and I do mean *all*.

Roger Williams—what is there not to like about Roger Williams? He was always stirring the pot and agitating those in power. He was so consistent with what he believed and taught. It's easy to talk about freedom for yourselves, but to give that same freedom to those with whom you definitively disagree, well, this is the true definition of freedom. And old Roger, he always felt free to try new things, to change for what he considered to be something better, even if it meant leaving the Baptists to become a Seeker. Baptist churches have expressed our freedom time and time again throughout our history, seeking to be God's people wherever we live. We Baptists love our history. But we build upon our history by constantly changing so that we can be relevant in an ever-evolving environment. Our freedom under God and the Constitution liberates us to change when necessary.

And Elder John Leland, what a character and what a patriot! "Give me liberty or give me death." Well, he didn't say this, but he could have. Even James Madison had to be impressed by the radical Baptists of his day. And he was! And because of these Orange County Baptists, Madison made a huge difference in guaranteeing all kinds of freedoms as a part of the Constitution.

But you know what? To find the true author of our freedom we have to go all the way back to Jesus. The apostle Paul, in a moment of heated debate with some real legalistic believers, wrote in his letter to the churches of Galatia, "For freedom Christ set us free." Quite possibly the one constant in who we have been and who we are as Baptists is that we have the freedom to build upon our past, as well as the liberty to grow, and to learn, and to keep on changing. As long as we believe and practice this freedom, we shall truly be free. Our name may be Baptist, but our friends (and maybe even our opponents) should call us "Liberty!"

Allow me to conclude with a few final thoughts based upon my fellow Baptists who have spoken today. I repeat that my name is Baptist! But you can call me "Liberty!" In the history of England and the United States, and throughout the world, we people called Baptists have been among the most vocal and aggressive groups to demand liberty for all people. We have consistently demanded freedom for all groups and individuals, including freedom to believe, to worship, and to practice their faith without support or opposition by any government. We have a special reason to celebrate our liberties every Fourth of July. Not only do we celebrate democratic freedom when we remember the writing and adoption of the Declaration of Independence; we also celebrate Christian freedom and our distinctive Baptist freedom.

A great irony of history is the fact that Thomas Jefferson and his good friend, yet political rival, John Adams both passed away on July 4, 1826, fifty years to the day after the adoption of our nation's foundational document. The demand for freedom had lasted half a century. It still stands. So, on July 4 of this year, be reminded anew of this same Declaration of Independence, which provided the foundation for your Constitution, and of your Bill of Rights, which guarantees your precious freedoms. But don't forget us Baptists, who for more than four centuries have demanded freedom for ourselves and all others in matters of religion

But be warned. Today, you Baptists are experiencing an erosion of freedom by those who should love it, defend it, and practice it. Freedom is nothing more than a slogan if you don't respect it, encourage it, and live it. These are the best ways to defend your freedoms!

So, celebrate the Fourth of July, one of the most consequential dates in the history of your nation. But please remember what I have said. Remember with courage your Founding Fathers who demanded freedom, fought for freedom, obtained freedom, and preserved freedom, beginning with the Declaration of Independence in 1776, then the Constitution in 1787, and the Bill of Rights in 1791, which established and legalized universal freedom for all citizens of the nation.

And when people ask, "Who are you?" tell them your name, tell them you are Baptist, or tell them you are Christian, or tell them you are simply a citizen of the United States of America. Then tell them your friends know you as "Liberty!"

EXTRA OPTIONS

Invocation: Our God, on this Lord's Day we come together as a free people. Free in faith, free in worship, free in our religion, free as citizens of this land. Let us depart in gratitude and humility for the gift of liberty in our nation and in our faith. Renew in all of our people a respect of and a quest for religious liberty for everyone, and political freedom for all. Make us truly free by exercising our freedoms and defending the liberty for our fellow citizens. Help us to live out our freedom in faith, with hope, and through love, and lead us to defend justice, display courage, and demonstrate a spirit of acceptance and understanding of all.

As Christ, our liberator, has set us free, let us truly live free. For we petition you in his name, Amen!

Benediction: Ask the people to repeat responsively the First Amendment to the Constitution of the United States of America: "Congress shall make no law / respecting an establishment of religion, / or prohibiting the free exercise thereof; / or abridging the freedom of speech, / or of the press; / or the right of the people peaceably to assemble, / and to petition the Government for a redress of grievances."

APPENDIX 1: ETERNAL WORD, O WORD OF GOD – HYMN

Words by Slayden Yarbrough (Tune: St. Anne: "O God, Our Help in Ages Past")

Eternal Word, O Word of God
Which guides our thoughts and deeds
That speaks of love, conveys our hopes
And meets our daily needs

Eternal word, Creative Word
Burst forth at first day's light
O Precious Word, God's Holy word
Bless us with truth and right

O Word of God incarnate come
To dwell within this place
To care, to teach, to die, to rise
To meet us face to face

O written Word, O precious Word
Passed down through every age
Portray anew, your message true
Revealed upon each page

O Word proclaimed throughout the world
In every tongue and land

O Living Word, O Holy Word
Henceforth, will ever stand

O Word revealed in daily walk
Made known to all who see
Who feel your touch and know your love
When sanctified in me.

APPENDIX 2: I AM CHRISTMAS: A DRAMATIC READING – by Slayden A. Yarbrough

I Am Christmas – An Introduction – Pastor

I Am Christmas – The Prophets – Pastor

"O Come, O Come, Emmanuel" vs. 1 – Song Leader

I Am Christmas – Caesar Augustus – Actor

I Am Christmas – Elizabeth – Actor

I Am Christmas – Bethlehem – Actor

"O Little Town of Bethlehem" vs. 1 – Song Leader

I Am Christmas – The Innkeeper – Actor

"Away in the Manger" vss. 1 & 2 – Song Leader

I Am Christmas – Mary – Actor

"Silent Night" vss. 1 & 2 – Song Leader

I Am Christmas – The Star – Actor

"It Came upon a Midnight Clear" vs. 1 – Song Leader

We Are Christmas – Shepherds in the Fields – Actor

"O Holy Night" – solo – Song Leader

I Am Christmas – The Three Wise Men – Actor

"We Three Kings" vs. 2 – Song Leader

I Am Christmas – Herod the Great – Actor

"O Come All Ye Faithful" vss. 1 & 2 – Song Leader

I Am Christmas – The Challenge – Pastor

"Angels We Have Heard on High" vss. 1 & 3 – Song Leader

Responsive Reading: We Are Christmas – Pastor and the People

PASTOR: I am Christmas. I am a child of God. I am hope, and faith, and joy, and peace. And so are you, if you know and understand and accept this great gift of God to the entire world, which you celebrate on Christmas Day.

PEOPLE: We are Christmas.

PASTOR: We are Christmas!

PEOPLE: We are Christmas!

PASTOR: We all are children of God who give witness to the Christ child. We reflect his light in a darkened world.

PEOPLE: We are Christmas!

PASTOR: We sing of his joy when surrounded by sorrow and grief. We anticipate his hope for all who are hopeless. We share his gift to those who are in spiritual and physical need. We convey his love in an angry and volatile world. We are the Spirit of Christmas for this generation.

PEOPLE: We are Christmas!

PASTOR: We are Christmas and we rejoice in God's grace, not just on this day, but every day.

ALL (PASTOR AND PEOPLE): We are Christmas! We are light! We are joy! We are hope! We say again for all to hear, we are Christmas!

"Go Tell It on the Mountain" – chorus, repeat – Song Leader

A Christmas Prayer – Pastor

APPENDIX 3: INSTRUCTIONS FOR DRAMATIC READING

Thanks to all of you for volunteering to be a part of the dramatic reading in today's program. A few suggestions as you prepare: Make sure you speak directly into the microphone. Remember, even though you may be reading your part, in actuality you are speaking to the congregation and telling them about your character, so make sure you go over your part sufficiently to where you are thoroughly familiar with it.

As you prepare, please take your time. You are not trying to rush through your part. When you begin, take a good look at the congregation before you say anything. Then, clearly and loudly (don't shout but use your best strong voice), begin. Most of you will start by introducing yourself (character). Pause, then proceed. Speak or read in short segments. I usually insert slash marks (/) between places where I want to pause. Again, take your time. Continue to make eye contact. If you are asking a question, pause to let the congregation think about it. Not too long, just enough time for the question to soak in.

Be prepared to move to the microphone as soon as it is time for your part. You will not be announced. Have fun and if you have any questions, don't hesitate to ask.

Endnotes

1 New International Version (NIV)

2 Statistics are for 2019.in https://www.wycliffe.org.uk/resources/press-releases/latest-bible-translation-figures/

3 https://www.preteristarchive.com/ChurchHistory/0325_eusebius_history.html, chapter XXXIX, number 15.

4New American Standard Bible (NASB)

CPSIA information can be obtained
at www.ICGtesting.com
Printed in the USA
LVHW050206041120
670658LV00007B/127